بِسْمِ اللهِ الرَّحْمٰنِ الرَّحِيْمِ

Presented to ....

....

From ....

Date ....

Also by Maulana Wahiduddin Khan

The Moral Vision
Islam As It Is
Religion and Science
A Treasury of the Qur'an
Woman in Islamic Shari'ah
Islam: Creator of the Modern Age
Words of the Prophet Muhammad
Islam: The Voice of Human Nature
An Islamic Treasury of Virtues
Woman Between Islam and Western Society
Islam and the Modern Man
Muhammad: A Prophet for All Humanity
Muhammad: The Ideal Character
Islam and Peace
Principles of Islam
The Call of the Qur'an
The Qur'an: An Abiding Wonder
The Quran For All Humanity
The Good Life
The Way to Find God
The Teachings of Islam
The Garden of Paradise
The Fire of Hell
Indian Muslims
Tabligh Movement
Man Know Thyself
Polygamy and Islam
Hijab in Islam
Concerning Divorce
Uniform Civil-Code
Introducing Islam
God Arises

The Moral Vision

Maulana Wahiduddin Khan

Goodword
B·O·O·K·S

Translated by Farida Khanam

First published 1999
© Goodword Books 2000
Reprint 2000

Distributed by
GOODWORD BOOKS
1, Nizamuddin West Market
New Delhi 110 013
Tel. 462 5454, 461 1128
Fax 469 7333, 464 7980
E-mail: skhan@vsnl.com
Website: www.alrisala.org

Contents

Publishers Note	9
Human Potential	10
Moon Mission	11
Our Potential is our Wealth	13
The Life Force	14
Motion and Direction	16
Hasten Slowly	18
Having the Courage to Err	19
The Order of Nature	20
Working Together	22
Working on the Individual	24
Idleness	25
The Making and Breaking of History	27
Some Make Themselves, Others Make History	29
Education	30
The Psychology of Success	32
Per Ardua ad Astra (Through Hardship to the Stars)	33
Try, Try, Try Again	35
Our 'Turnkey' Civilization	37
Getting off to a Good Start	39
Planting the Tree of the Nation	41
Bearing Fruit	42
Good Egg	44
Road Block	45
Unlocking the Gates to Success	46
Working Together	48
In the Nick of Time	50

The Human Personality	51
Concentration	53
A Shaft of Light	54
Narrow-Mindedness	56
Another Day! How Wonderful	57
When One is Broken in Two	59
Destined for Great Deeds	60
In Giving We Receive	62
How Do You Win the Nobel Prize?	63
Gerard of Cremona	64
Trust is Golden	66
The Secret of Success	67
Reading the Signs	69
Aiming Directly at the Target	71
Teacher Tree	73
Starting from Scratch	74
Admitting One's Faults	75
No End to Possibilities	76
Perseverance	78
Working in Unison	79
Unforeseen Circumstances	81
Capability and Alertness	82
Talking Tall	84
A Life-time of Devotion	85
Right Man—Right Results	86
Man's True Purpose in Life	87
The Bigger the Better	90
No Half Measures	91
The Learner-Teacher	92
The Beginning of a New Era	94
Super Performers	95
The Purpose of Life	96

Reciprocity	99
Through Fire and Water	100
Patience, Perseverance and Compassion	101
What Must Be Known Before One Can Understand	102
Disadvantage Turned to Advantage	104
Reply without Reaction	105
Finders, not Losers	106
Disunity: The Enemy's Weapon	108
An Eye for a Talent	109
Labour of a Lifetime	111
Quiet Endeavour	113
Overcoming Handicaps	115
The Virtues of Dependability	116
The Japanese Experience	117
The Law of Nature	120
The Root Cause of Riots	121
Going Places on Home Ground	123
Learning from Mistakes	124
Nightly Preparation for a Mighty Task	125
Accepting Defeat	127
Total Involvement	128
Progress in the Long Haul	130
The Greatest Asset	131
All the Blood of One's Body	133
After Being Broken	135
Recognizing Oneself	136
Social Behaviour	139
Life's Labours are Never Lost	143
An Economic Pearl Harbour	144
Having One's Share	147
Message Without Words	148
Working One's Way Up	150

Warding off Danger	151
Aiming High	153
The Flight of the Bee	155
Teaching the Teachers	156
Keeping Calm in the Face of Adversity	158
Seeking the Right Alternatives	160
In Giving We Receive	162
Beware of Negative Thinking	164
Ducking Below the Waves	166
Constructive Temperament	167
Perseverance Pays	169
Ease Always Comes After Hardship	170
Making the Extra Effort	172
Big-Heartedness	173
There is Always a Way	177
Proceeding with Caution	178
The First Emigration	180
Muslim Journalism	181
A Practical Solution	183
The Will to Unite	184
Doing One's Bit	186
Broken Pledges	187
Dreams and Success	189
Ethics and Technology	190
The More Hurry, the Less Speed	192
God Helps Those Who Help Themselves	193
Negligence: A Moral Deficiency	196
A Lesson from a Tiger	198
Realizing One's Own Shortcomings	200
Character Builds the Nation	202
How to Lead, Even in Defeat	203
History Speaks	205

Publisher's Note

This anthology of articles by Maulana Wahiduddin Khan is designed to illustrate the science of life which the author has derived from one of the basic principles of the Qur'an: "Every hardship comes with ease." (94:5-6). In his view, failure in life is a common occurrence, but that coupled with a positive attitude, it can be transformed into success. Failure, on the other hand, coupled with a negative attitude is again failure. The author gives examples from daily life. Supported by relevant quotations from the Qur'an and the sayings of the Prophet Muhammad, to show that there is no end to the possibilities of success in life for the individual who can take a lesson form failure. He also cautions that life's tribulations must be faced with patience, perservance and compassion.

All the articles in this anthology have appeared from time to time in *Al-Risala*.

Human Potential

In the Ohio University of the U.S.A. there is a department known as the Disaster Research Centre. It was established in 1963, and has so far studied over one hundred different calamities affecting human beings on a vast scale. It was discovered that at moments of crisis, an extraordinary new potential develops in people which saves them from succumbing to disasters and their aftermath. In 1961, for example, Texas was struck by a severe coastal tempest, but less than half of the inhabitants opted to vacate the area. Over 50 percent of them had the confidence to stay on in spite of the storm warnings issued to them four days in advance. Subsequently, in 1971, a big dam was weakened considerably following an earthquake, which seriously endangered the lives of 70,000 people, but at that very critical time only 7 percent of the population chose to leave their hearths and homes.

Such research has also revealed that the victims of such disasters still maintain high hopes for the future. The citizens of the two affected areas of Texas, having witnessed the destruction caused by horrible floods, were interviewed about what they felt were their future prospects. Surprisingly, less then ten percent expressed apprehension and misgivings. The rest of them, irrespective of the large-scale destruction, were hopeful about their future. The above-mentioned institute concluded the report of the research it had conducted on disasters by saying, "The reality of events suggests that human beings are amazingly controlled and resilient in the face of adversity. Perhaps heroism, not panic or shock, is the right word to describe their most common behaviour in times of disaster." The Creator has endowed His creature man with extraordinary capabilities, one of which is his capacity to plan his life anew with tremendous vigour, even when threatened with total annihilation. Man can do more than compensate for his losses. The discovery of this natural, hidden potential in man serves to teach a great lesson, that is, that no individual, whether singly or as part of a group, who suffers trials and tribulations, should ever waste a moment's time in lamenting and grieving over his losses. Instead, he should press God-given capabilities into service to reconstruct his life. It is quite possible that the very circumstances in which he seemed to be heading towards complete annihilation, could serve to unfold a new and brighter phase of his existence.

Moon Mission

American Astronaut, Neil Armstrong, stepped on to the moon for the first time in July, 1969. The moment he set his foot on the moon, the control mission in American received these words uttered by him :

"That's one small step for a man, one giant leap for mankind."

Armstrong and his two colleagues were selected from amongst the top 30 astronauts of the U.S.A. He possessed to a very high degree all those qualities which were necessary for this difficult, historic mission—extraordinary skill in flying, intelligence, strength, ability to absorb information, mental and emotional balance and the courage to accept challenges unhesitatingly. Once selected, he had to undergo rigorous training, for instance, having to remain in deep water for long periods so that he would become used to weightlessness. So that he could deal with every possible emergency, he did elaborate courses in astronomy, space flight, rocket flight, the physics of the moon, etc.—all with the help of computerized space data.

The 3100 ton Apollo 11 seemed a giant. It was as high as a 36 storey building, having 8 million parts and 91 engines installed in it. On the top was the comparatively small machine, the Columbia, in which the astronauts were seated to set off on their historic journey.

The space machine was duly blasted off, circling the earth for two and a half hours. Then its speed increased to 403 miles per minute and on reaching an altitude of 3000 miles the Columbia separated from the rest of the machines. It was so equipped that the seating space for the astronauts was only as much as in an ordinary taxi. Finally they alighted on the moon from where they gathered 46 pounds of moon-earth, leaving equipment worth 5 Lakh pounds behind them. They also left their foot prints on its surface which, hopefully will remain intact for half a million years.

It was only after such highly elaborate preparations that the "small step" could be taken which was going to result in such a "giant leap" for mankind".

Our Potential is our Wealth

Psychologists have estimated that man puts to use only ten percent of the abilities with which he is born. Professor William James of Harvard University has very aptly observed, "What we ought to be, we are not ready to be." In spite of the inborn qualities nature has endowed us with, the successes which should have been ours in this world keep eluding us for the simple reason that we quite unthinkingly consent to lead inferior lives. Then, discontented, we put the blame on others for not giving us our due. But it is inside ourselves that we should look if we are to find the reasons for life's deficiencies. Constantly viewing others with envy and a sense of grievance will lead us nowhere, and can turn us into our own worst enemies. The fact should be faced fairly and squarely that it is only if we exploit our own potential to the full that we shall meet with success. Any other course will lead to failure.

It is essential, however, to determine at the outset whether our efforts are directed at worthwhile objectives. Without proper direction our potential will be wasted.

In ancient times and even up to mediaeval times, gold being greatly prized, one of the great preoccupations of the 'scientists' of those days was to convert base metals into gold. Dreams of instant wealth drove innumerable people over the centuries to superhuman efforts. But all this expenditure of time, money and energy was in vain, for death always overtook them before they could achieve anything. It never seemed to occur to any of them that these metals with which they worked had a different and greater potential than anyone could ever have imagined. Iron, for example, was convertible, not into gold, but into machinery, and could be used as a versatile building material of great strength. In the world of today, western nations, having learnt these secrets and directed their energies towards building up the relative technology, have succeeded in acquiring far greater wealth than mere silver and gold.

The Life Force

A creeper growing in a courtyard once had the misfortune to have its roots and branches buried under mounds of earth and rubble when the house was undergoing repairs. Later, when the courtyard was cleaned up, the owner of the house cut away the creeper, which had been badly damaged, and even pulled out its roots so that it would not grow again. The whole courtyard was then laid with bricks and cemented over.

A few weeks later, something stirred at the place where the creeper had been rooted out. The bricks heaved upwards at one point as though something were pushing them from below. This appeared very strange, but was dismissed as being the burrowings of rats or mice. The riddle was solved when some of the bricks were removed, and it was discovered that the creeper had started growing again, although in a sadly distorted form. As it happened, not all of its roots had been pulled out, and when the time of the year came around for them to grow, life began to stir within them and they pushed their way up through the cement to the sunlight. It is one of nature's miracles that these tender leaves and buds, which can be so easily crushed to a pulp between finger and thumb, can summon up such strength as to force their way through bricks and cement.

The owner of the house then regretted having attempted to take the creeper's life. He remarked, "It is just as if it were appealing to me for the right to grow. Now I certainly won't stand in its way." And so saying, he removed some more of the bricks so that it would grow unhindered. In less than a year's time, a fifteen-foot creeper was flourishing against the courtyard wall at the exact point from which it had been so unceremoniously 'uprooted.'

A mountain, despite its great height and girth, cannot remove so much as a pebble from its flanks. But these tiny, tender buds of the tree can crack a cemented floor and sprout up through it. Whence such power? The source of its energy is the mysterious phenomenon of our world called life. Life is an astonishing, ongoing process of this universe—a force which will claim its rights in this world, and, even when uprooted, it continues to exist, albeit dormant, at one place or the other and reappears the moment it finds the opportunity. Just when people have come to the conclusion that, because there is nothing visible on the surface, life must be at an end, that is just when it rears its head from the debris.

Motion and Direction

A western thinker once commented, "You have removed most of the road blocks to success when you have learnt the difference between motion and direction."

One intrinsic quality of activity is movement. When you are walking, driving, riding a bicycle, galloping along on horseback or roaring along on a motorcycle, you are moving. But in what direction? Are you moving towards your destination, or away from it? The actual motion in both cases seems to be no different in quality.

The great difference between the two is that the former brings you ever nearer to your destination, while the latter takes you further and further away from it—leaving you where ? Nowhere. At least, nowhere worth going. It is direction that is all-important. Even if we only get on to the slow-moving bullock cart or a cycle rickshaw, we shall do better than a jet plane which has no sense of direction.

Both in our private lives and social existence, it is imperative that we take stock of our means and resources and then set off in the right direction, if, sooner or later, we are to reach our destination.

Often people launch themselves on careers, plunging headlong into them, without giving due thought to their actual capacities and to whether they have any real potential which can be developed. At times they are led astray by trivial considerations, ill-founded opinions and overwhelming emotions, and rush heedlessly into whatever first comes their way. When the result is not what they had anticipated, they fall to complaining against others, lamenting their losses and failures and claiming that it was due to the prejudices of others that they had had to suffer frustrations and that their careers had come to naught. Had they given more profound thought to the matter, they would have realised that the fault lay in their own ill-judged planning or even total aimlessness. Had they started out in the right direction, others would not then have had the opportunity to place obstacles in their path and turn their successes into failures.

Hasten Slowly

"A young man once came to a venerable master and asked, 'How long will it take to reach enlightenment?' The master said, 'Ten years.' The young man blurted out, 'So long!' The master said, 'No, I was mistaken. It will take you twenty years.' The young man asked, 'Why do you keep adding to it!' The master answered, 'Come to think of it, in your case it will probably be 30 years.' (Philip Kapleau, *Readers Digest*, 1983)

A goal can be achieved in the course of ten years, but you want to attain in just ten days. This means that you want to reach your destination in tremendous leaps and bounds. But there is an old saying: "The more hurry, the less speed."

A traveller who wants to dash straight as an arrow, without allowing time for twists and turns, will collide with many obstacles in his headlong flight. Far from reaching his destination faster, he will surely come to grief and fall by the wayside. He shall then have to retrace his steps to the starting point, heal his wounds and only then set forth again. All of this will take time, precious time—time which should have been spent on the onward journey. Had he proceeded in a normal, unhurried way, he would have reached his destination all in good time.

Just as it is wrong to delay, it is equally wrong to be in too much of a hurry. All work can be completed in due course. To delay work is idle and irresponsible, but to do it with unseemly and unwarrantable haste is a sign of crass impatience. In the world of God, where each event has its allotted time, both extremes are doomed to failure.

Having the Courage to Err

Two friends, Ahmed and Iqbal, both lived in the same city. Ahmed was a graduate, while Iqbal's education had not gone beyond the eighth standard. It happened once that Iqbal had to go to an office on business and was accompanied by his friend, Ahmed. When the business had been transacted, and they were both coming out of the office, Ahmed said to Iqbal, "You were speaking such horrible English! With such bad English, I would never have dared to open my mouth!" Iqbal was not the slightest bit disconcerted at being so roundly criticized. Exuding confidence, he said, "Speak wrong so that you can speak right!" Then he added, "Although you are a graduate and I have not got any degrees, you will soon find that I will start speaking in English and you will never be able to do so."

That was twenty years ago. Now Iqbal's words have come true. Ahmed is still at the stage he was at twenty years ago, but Iqbal, astonishingly, has made great progress. He now speaks English quite fluently and no one can fault him on grammar and pronunciation.

This daring attitude on the part of Iqbal certainly proved to be of great advantage to him for, at the outset of his career, he just owned a small shop in the city, whereas today, he runs a big factory.

The motto: "Speak wrong so that you can speak correct," has obviously in his case been the key to success. This principle on which Iqbal operated has a bearing not only on language but on all practical concerns in life. In the present world, the potentially successful are those who are possessed of courage, who advance fearlessly and take the initiative in the face of risks. Only those who have the courage to err will accomplish anything worthwhile in life. Those who are afraid of making mistakes will be left behind in the race of life, and their ultimate goals will recede further and further into the distance.

The Order of Nature

Try closing your room, going away, and returning after a few weeks. What do you find on your return? A thick layer of dust all over the room. This is so unpleasant that you don't feel like sitting in the room until it has been dusted. Equally upleasant is the dust blown in your face by a high wind, you find yourself longing for the wind to drop, so that there should be no more irritating dust.

But what is this dust that we find so annoying? It is in fact a loose surface layer of fertile soil, the very substance which enables the growth of all forms of vegetables, fruits and cereals. If this soil did not lie on the face of the earth, it would be impossible for us to live on the earth at all.

It is this same dust that makes the earth's atmosphere dense enough for water to vaporize, forming clouds which produce torrents of water to revive and replenish the earth. Without rain, there would be no life on earth, and rain is only possible because of the dust in the earth's atmosphere.

The redness of the sky which we see at sunrise and sunset is also due to the presence of dust in the atmosphere. In this way dust, besides possessing multiple practical benefits, also contributes to the beauty of the world.

From this straightforward example we can see how God has placed unpleasant things alongside the pleasant things of life. Just as the rose bush, along with its exquisite flowers, also possesses piercing thorns, so also does life contain an amalgam of both pleasing and displeasing objects. This is the way God has created the world. There is nothing for us to do but to fit in with this order of nature that He has laid down. Much as we may try, it is impossible for us to have things any other way.

To complain about things, then, is a fruitless exercise.

If one wants to complain, one is sure to find plenty to complain about in life. The intelligent thing to do is to forget the unpleasant things which are a part and parcel of life, bury grudges, and carry on seeking to fulfill one's true purpose in life.

Working Together

One particular quality of true believers has been pinpointed in the Qur'an. It is that when they are with the Prophet—or in other words the person responsible for Muslims' affairs—"on a matter requiring collective action, they do not depart until they have asked for his leave..." (Qur'an, 24:62). Here collective action means any activity involving a group of people working together. And the "asking of leave" is indicative of the wider spirit in which the work is done—a spirit of deep commitment, like the commitment one feels to some personal work.

A high degree of motivation is required for a person to become so deeply involved in a task that he will not leave it until the work in hand has been accomplished. Such motivation is inherent in work involving personal profit: it is in one's own interest to see the work through to the bitter end, and so one does so. One is moved by a sense of personal responsibility: if one does not accomplish the task oneself, who will do if for one? With work involving a group of people, on the other hand, one tends to lay the onus on other people. If I don't carry on, on thinks, there are plenty of others who will continue in my place. Seeing that there is no personal profit to be gained from the work in hand, one tends to see it as a burden best laid on others' shoulders. Only when one has come to think of the common good as one's own good, of the profit of society as one's own profit, will one become fully committed to collective work. Such commitment requires, above all, a deep sense of social consciousness; it requires one to be oriented towards the needs of the community, as anyone would normally be oriented to cater for his own needs.

A Muslim is required to possess just such a sense of social consciousness, moving him to throw himself heart and soul into collective Islamic work, whenever such work is required of him. Then, when he has involved himself in it, he will see it through to the final stage. When he takes leave from the authority under whose direction he is working, he does not do so in order to desert the cause to which he is committed; rather, he has some valid reason for going away, and will return as soon as circumstances allow. For this reason the Qur'an says that, if possible, such requests should be granted. But both the request, and the granting of it, should be made in the correct spirit, with both parties praying for the other, even as they part.

Working on the Individual

A man was riding his bicycle one day when all of a sudden his brake jammed. Luckily there was a cycle repair-shop nearby, so he took his bike there to have it fixed. Thinking that the mechanic would fix the brake at the point where it was jammed, the cyclist was surprised to see him tap away with a small hammer at a completely different place. Before he was able to express his surprise, however, the mechanic handed the bike over. "That's fixed it. You can take it away now," he said. And off the cyclist rode, with his bike once again running smoothly.

What was true of this bicycle is true also of human society. When there is something wrong with society, people usually jump to the conclusion that where the malaise lies, there also lies the cure. But this is not case. Usually the root of the malaise lies in a different place, far away from the symptoms. Until the cause is removed, the malaise itself will not go away.

For instance, there might be a lack of solidarity in society, or one's people may be the victims of oppression. Maybe society is beset with an atmosphere of intrigue, with the result that its voice carries no weight in the world. Detecting these symptoms, one who determines to right the ills of society might well think that the cure lies in calling meeting and conventions in order to bring people together, feeding them emotional speeches and passing high-sounding resolutions, and so on.

But this is not the way to cure the actual ills of society. To do so, one has to work on the cause, not the symptoms, for usually one will find that while a problem seems to be afflicting one part of society, the cure lies elsewhere. If there is a lack of solidarity, for instance, the reason for this is the failure of individuals to stand together. It is the individual, then, who has to be worked on. Solidarity has to be achieved at an individual level before it can come about in society. For it is a law of nature, and human society, that for a tree to bear good fruit, it is the seed, not the fruit itself, that has to be improved.

Idleness

The second Caliph, Umer ibn Khattab, often used to express his sense of disillusionment about people he had come to like, when, on further acquaintance with them he discovered them to be idle. "On learning that he does not work, he appears to me of no value (he has debased himself in my eyes)."

Whichever way you look at idleness, there is no gainsaying the fact that it is a great evil, causing one to fritter away one's best talents and leaving one unqualified to face life. A student who is too lazy to study cannot ever hope to acquire knowledge, or have his critical faculties sharpened in any way, and his failure in examinations will leave him without the 'paper' qualifications which is the 'Open Sesame' to good jobs. Without the necessary groundwork, he will find himself leading a vacant existence, simply drifting from pillar to post. Even people who have managed to qualify themselves suitably cannot afford to rest on their laurels. When the period of education is over, it is equally necessary to be consistently hard-working. Many make the excuse between the receipt of a degree and entry into a profession that they are waiting for the right job to come along. But one cannot go on waiting forever, simply idling away one's time.

Sometimes one inadvertently slips into idle ways because there are no economic pressures in one's life. Those who inherit legacies, or have property or investments which bring them some return are an easy prey to idleness. But this is no existence for a human being. Anyone who allows the poison of idleness to creep into his system might as well be dead.

Either one must opt for a regular job, which brings one a suitable income and keeps one mentally healthy, so that one never becomes a financial or emotional burden on anyone else, or, if one is financially independent, one should turn one's attention to higher things, pursue noble ends, serve worthy causes and keep oneself fruitfully occupied day in and day out. A person with no sense of commitment is only living on the fringes of existence. He is out of touch with reality and will soon lapse into utter degeneracy. No really superior being has ever been found among the ranks of the idle.

As the old saying goes, the Devil finds work for idle hands.

The Making and Breaking of History

According to B.Tuchman, "history is the unfolding of miscalculation." In other words, history usually develops in a manner quite contrary to people's expectations. While events are unfolding, observers may pass judgement on the course they are taking; but the course of history defies all prediction, and in the end things turn out quite differently from what people had initially expected.

To take an example from Islamic history, in the year 6AH the Treaty of Hudaybiyah was signed between the Prophet Muhammad and the Quraysh of Mecca. At that time the Quraysh were one in thinking that the Muslims had signed their own writ of destruction, for they accepted peace on terms which were clearly favourable to the Quraysh. Yet afterwards it transpired that this apparent defeat contained the seeds of a great victory for the Muslims. The same thing has happened time and time again throughout history. In 1945, when atombombs were dropped on the cities of Hiroshima and Nagasaki in Japan, it seemed to the Americans as if Japan would lie in ruins for several decades to come. Yet this was not to be: now, just forty years after the event, Japan stands at the pinnacle of her economic strength, the leading industrial power in the world.

This goes to show that it is not man who fashions his own history; in truth, it is God who fashions human history in accordance with His own will. It is not people or events who control history, it is God. History may take place before our eyes, in the material world, but the course it takes is determined from the super-natural world which lies beyond our vision and perception.

Those who have been written off as spent forces can take solace from this fact of history. Experience shows that sparks erupt from volcanoes that have lain inactive for years. In this world the very annihilation and destruction of something means that it is ready to arise and take its place as a new power on earth; a force which is spent turns into a living force.

One should never lose hope because of the dismal course events appear to be taking. When the pages of history turn, events may turn out to have been leading in a direction quite contrary to all our expectations.

Some Make Themselves, Others Make History

There are two types of people in this world—the self-making type and the history-making type. The aim of those who are self-making is to serve themselves, whereas history-making people seek to serve humanity as a whole.

The attention of a self-making person revolves around himself. He hovers around those areas where his own self-interest is likely to be served; where there is no profit to be gained for himself, he does not care to venture. His heart flutters with excitement when he is set to make some gain, but if there is nothing to be gained, no excitement is aroused within him. Personal gain is uppermost in his mind; he will sacrifice everything in order to achieve it. He abides neither by promise nor by principle. Free of the influence of both moral exigencies and the needs of humanity, he can put everything aside in pursuit of his own ends. All other considerations fade into insignificance as he relentlessly seeks to fulfill his selfish desires.

A history-making person is quite different. Emerging from his own shell, he lives not for himself but for a higher purpose. What matters to him is principle, not profit. He cares not whether he himself wins or loses ; what is of importance to him is that his ideal should be served. It is as if he has detached himself from his own person and pinned his flag to the needs of humanity as a whole.

In order to become a history-making person there is one thing that has to be done: one has to stop being self-making. As soon as a person effaces himself, he becomes capable of building for the future of humanity. Such a person lays personal grievances to one side. As his own self-interest and ambitions evaporate before his eyes, he shows no reaction, as if all this were not happening to him at all.

It is people such as these who are destined to forge human history. They are the ones who, of their own free will, are concerned about the rest of humanity; they have no rights to be safeguarded; they have only responsibilities, which they discharge whatever the cost to themselves.

Education

Knowledge is of two distinct kinds: that which we have been blessed with in the Qur'an and the Hadith, and that which we acquire as a result of our own research and endeavour. The first kind acquaints us with our Lord, and makes plain the issues to be faced in the everlasting world which awaits us after death. More important, it shows us how, in the course of our present life, we may prepare ourselves to meet those issues. The second kind of knowledge provides solutions to the social and economic problems which we encounter in everyday life.

It is imperative that Muslims should seek both forms of knowledge, but they should never lose sight of the fact that they vary considerably in importance. Their primary aim in life should be a knowledge of the Qur'an and the Hadith, while the acquisition of a knowledge of the other sciences should come about as a matter of worldly necessity. Without a knowledge of religion, what must be done in this world to earn an everlasting reward, will constantly elude one's understanding, and it goes without saying that one can never then consider oneself a Muslim in the true sense of the word.

The secular sciences guide us only in worldly matters, giving us instruction in the agricultural, industrial and civic practicalities of life. But it is the Qur'an and Hadith which set our feet on the path to eternal development. Clearly, it is just as important for Muslims as it is for anyone else to study various branches of knowledge, but they must distinguish between ultimate objectives and adventitious necessity. Muslims must not only study the Qur'an and the Hadith, but must be keenly aware that the real reasons for studying them are very different from those which prompt them to seek worldly knowledge: they must constantly bear in mind also that religious knowledge take moral priority over all other forms of knowledge.

The Psychology of Success

The World champions often possess equal physical strength and capabilities, and receive training of an almost equal standard. Then why does one win and another lose? This question has been a topic of research in America for the past three years. The report of the group of scientists working on this has recently been published.

They chose the top international wrestlers and made comparisons of their physical strength and psychological reserves. They found out that there is one marked difference between the winners and the losers in world competitions. It is not a physical difference, yet it plays the most crucial role in winning or losing a competition. The experts discovered that the winners were more conscientious and in control of themselves than the losers. The report is summed up as follows:

"Losers tended to be more depressed and confused before competing, while the winners were positive and relaxed."(*The Times of India,* 26 July, 1981). This applies equally to the broader field of life. In life when two individuals or two groups confront one another, their victory or defeat does not depend so much on material resources as on intellectual and psychological reserves.

The conviction that one's goals are worthwhile, the

observation of discipline with no contradiction between words and thoughts, cool thinking, even in times of crisis—all these are qualities of mind and heart which determine success, and obviate failure in the wider field of life.

Per Ardua ad Astra
(Through Hardship to the Stars)

According to an English scholar, Ian Nash, who spent eleven years in Japan making a detailed study of the language and nation, what shook the Japanese most profoundly was not upheavals in politics, but the great Kanto earthquake, which devastated the whole of the most populated eastern part of Japan on the first of September, 1923. Another terrible blow was the reduction of two of the great cities of Japan to smouldering mounds of waste by the dropping of atomic bombs. This lead to the ultimate defeat of Japan in the Second World War in 1945.

One might imagine that any country which has been dealt such shattering blows would never be able to rise again from its ashes. But this is far from being true, for Japan has not only rehabilitated itself, but now figures most prominently of all on the world commercial and industrial scene. Japan has became a great hive of technological activity in spite of having launched itself on an industrial course long after Britain, Europe and America. This is all the more remarkable, considering that Japan has none of the natural resources that the older established industrial nations have, buried right there in their own soil just waiting to be extracted.

In man's life the most important thing is the will to act. Had the Japanese succumbed to a sense of loss and frustration, and frittered their energies away in futile political protest, their country would have been doomed to decline and ruination. But, as it was, they conquered any sense of victimization they might have had and set about reconstructing their national life with a will and a way. Although earthquakes had brought them death and destruction, they had also galvanized them into building their lives afresh.

In such situations of grim affliction, provided one has the will, all one's hidden potential and latent faculties are brought into play. One can think better, plan more successfully and make the greater efforts needed to bring one's plans to fruition. One who lacks the will to improve his life is just like an idling motor which is going nowhere.

Experience has shown also that complacency and a sense of comfort can be even greater vitiating factors in man's progress through life than devastation and despair. This does not mean that adversity by itself is beneficial. No. It is simply the spark which ignites the fuel of man's soul and drives him on to greater things. It is the mainspring of his initiative and the force which propels him relentlessly forward. In the face of adversity his hidden capacities come to the fore and it is possible for him to reach undreamt of heights. But first and foremost there has to be the *will* to do so. There has to be the *will* to stop wallowing in self-pity and to get up and take action.

It is not ease, but effort, not facility, but difficulty which make a man what he is.

Try, Try, Try Again

A young man who was employed as an ordinary worker in a Bidi factory soon learnt the entire art of the business and set up his own factory. He initially invested only Rs. 5000 in his business, but then by dint of fifteen years' hard work, his business progressively increased until it expanded into a big factory. One day, narrating his life story to his friends, he said: "Just as a young child grows into boyhood after fifteen years, so does a business. I have not reached this stage in one day. It has been a fifteen-year struggle."

In truth every piece of work is accomplished in "fifteen" years, be it of an individual or a nation, be it a business or a social service. Those who long for a recipe for instant success are, in fact, living in a fool's paradise. It is all very well to *say* that a hop, step and jump can take you right to your destination. But as soon as one comes face to face with reality, one realises that this is just an illusion. Glenn Cunningham, a sportsman who became champion of the one-mile race, saw the school in which he was studying go up in flames. His own experience was terrible. His feet were so badly burnt that he could not even move his legs. The doctors lost all hope of his ever walking or running. They said that only a miracle could save him. Surprisingly Glenn Cunningham's incapacity excited in him a new zeal and eagerness to walk and run. All his mental faculties concentrated on his decision to walk. So he began to experiment with different kinds of exercises till he hit upon a novel idea. It was to drag himself along by holding on to the handle of a moving plough. When his feet could even so much as rest on the ground, he felt encouraged, and intensified his efforts. Finally, the miracle of which the doctors had so despaired, took place. The new technique was a tremendous success and, ultimately, he could not only walk, but could also run. Later he entered for a race. He set up a new record and became a champion of the one-mile race. But this grand success was not achieved in a few days. He had to spend "fifteen years" realizing his goal. Only after a fifteen year stint had it been possible for him to become a flat racing champion.

In truth, no success is possible in this world without working for "fifteen years." It is God alone who has the power to achieve instant success. But God has not created this world on the basis of instant success. Man must learn his lesson and should not fritter away his time in futile efforts. In this world of God, innumerable events are taking place, all of which are based on eternal, immutable laws. Not even a blade of grass grows here on the ground as a result of wishful thinking, not even an ant can manage to live by ignoring the realities of life. How is it possible then for man to change the divine laws? The only condition of success is continuous effort, that is, to make such unflagging efforts, are as essential to achieve the desired objectives in the world of God according to the law of God. By following the same principle we can achieve success in this world; it is the same principle which will bring us success in the next world.

Our 'Turnkey' Civilization

In the modern, industrial world, the term 'Turnkey Project' has come to be widely used. Ready-made houses and factories are made today in which everything is provided by the seller. The buyer has only to turn the key in order to use it. The behaviour of certain Muslims of the present day suggests that they think the world is theirs for taking, that God has handed it over to them ready-made and that all they have to do is 'turn the key' and everything and everyone will be ready to do their bidding.

Little do they realize how far this is from being the true state of affairs. This world, in reality, is one of vigorous action and keen competition, and no worthwhile position can be attained without working hard on every aspect of the project in hand, and no job is well done unless carried out with scrupulous care from beginning to end. Our very right to live has to be proved by competing with others. Only when we plunge wholeheartedly into the fray, can we hope to attain the place we desire in this world of cause and effect. There is no question of just 'turning the key'.

Muslims of the present day must learn before all else that they are at the beginning of history, and not the end. Everyone knows that this is January, 1986 and that for it to be December, 1986, we shall have to wait twelve months. The earth shall have to revolve on its axis 365 times and only then shall we come to the end of one year. This is common knowledge. But Muslims tend to overlook such obvious facts when it comes to the building of their nation. They have only just entered the first month, but they want to leap straight into the twelfth. They make no effort to lay the foundations of the homes they keep imagining, but already they want to stand on their rooftops. The very phrasing of their speeches and writings gives the impression that they have actually attained their objectives.

We should remember, first and foremost, that we can create a nation only if its inhabitants are imbued with a sense of purpose and, to that end, we must educate our people: they must have full knowledge of both the past and the present if they are to progress towards an ideal future. We have to inculcate in them the will to work unitedly in spite of their disagreements. We have to instill in them the courage to sacrifice their personal feelings and their short-term interests for long-term ones. Only then will it be possible to fashion history anew.

Getting off to a Good Start.

"Here are my entire life's savings." So saying, an elderly scholar, who had spent his whole life reading and writing, in the utmost simplicity, placed a cheque for Rs 10,000 in the hands of his newly-wed daughter and son-in-law. He explained that he had been able to save this amount out of his meagre income by living frugally and never wasting anything. "I could have spent all this on lavish wedding celebrations," he added, "but I preferred to hand it over to you young people so that you could make a good beginning in life."

The young couple were extremely grateful for this decision and lost no time in investing the money in a small business. To begin with they had to work very hard to make a success of it, and passed through various difficult stages. But they never lost courage, and a time eventually came when they had considerably increased their profits and were able to live a happy, comfortable life. Knowing, too, that their children's future was assured. But without the scholar's initial providence, foresight and courage in resisting public opinion, they might never have had the wherewithal to make a start in life at all and might well have ended their days in penury.

One's wedding is a very serious event in life, not just an occasion for senseless showing off. It is rather a day to shoulder life's responsibilities as mature, grown-up people and future parents. It is a day for a man and a woman to enter into a 'firm contract' (Qur'an, 4:21), not just an opportunity to impress friends, neighbours and relatives with one's spending ability. It is at all events advisable that the marriage ceremony should be simple and straightforward, thereby avoiding pointless expenditure. Before anyone spends his entire life's savings, on gaudy displays—for money, after all is hard earned and difficult to accumulate—he should reflect seriously on the above-mentioned incident.

All things considered, would it not be better to avoid ostentation altogether and to think of how best one can help the young couple concerned? If this practice were to become widely adopted, it would not only benefit young people in general, but would actually make a positive contribution to national construction. The millions of rupees which are habitually lavished on short-lived magnificence could then be channelized into areas of the national economy which are at present unfairly neglected, thus creating favourable conditions for general economic uplift.

Planting the Tree of the Nation

The former U.S. President, John F. Kennedy, referring to Lyautey, once remarked :

> "I once asked my gardener to plant a tree. The gardener objected that the tree was slow growing and would not reach maturity for a hundred years. I replied, "In that a case there is no time to lose, plant it in the afternoon..."
>
> *Chartered Account*, New Delhi, 79. (Supplement)

The growth and development of a nation is likewise a lengthy affair, and there has to be a tremendous input at both the individual and national levels before it finally bursts into blossom and finds the position of honour and glory that it merits in world affairs. But to one who points who out that no one can wait for a national policy to mature if it is going to take a hundred years, the only answer is : "In that case, we cannot afford to lose even a single moment. We must plant our 'tree' this very minute".

If it takes a mighty tree one hundred years to reach its full stature, whoever wishes to possess such a tree has no option but to tend it for that period. If instead of nurturing it with care and skill, people come out on to the streets and launch a strike campaign in the name of trees, or gather in some open place or march through the streets shouting slogans about it, they will never possess a single tree, less own an orchard.

Similarly, you cannot own a house by making eloquent speeches about the need for one. It would be the crassest stupidity to do so. Neither can a nation fortify itself by working miracles only in the field of politics. In the rarefied world of poetry, revolution can occur as a result of a mere play on words. A demagogue can make impassioned speeches and attract great crowds. But real results can be achieved only by long-term planning and continuing and dedicated effort.

Needless to say, the two great virtues which are indispensable in the struggle are patience and fortitude.

Bearing Fruit

The business of planting an orchard does not begin with the holding of an orchard conference. No, indeed. It begins by obtaining seedlings and providing every single one with such favourable conditions as will enable it to develop its potential and grow into a fully developed tree. When one has done this with innumerable seedlings, one can then expect to have an orchard.

In this respect, a nation is somewhat like an orchard. Build the individual and you build the nation. If hidden potential is to be developed, it takes education, encouragement, and the provision of a proper environment at an individual level very early on in the whole process, just as a sapling must be put into well prepared ground and given the right type and quantity of nutrients, water, sunlight, etc. If people are properly instructed, while they are still young and receptive and by people who adopt a caring, positive attitude, they develop a healthy awareness of what their commitments to society should be and what it means to be part of a nation. If callow youths are to be turned into real men, they have to have the feeling inculcated in them that to achieve positive ends they must continually keep up a peaceful and ameliorative struggle, one which will create harmony and eschew conflict, one which will solve, and not create problems for their fellow men.

Although we must accept the fact that this is a highly competitive world, there is nothing to prevent us from endeavouring to cooperate with and encourage cooperation from others. If we stand shoulder to shoulder with our fellow men in the face of the most heartless rivalries, there is no obstacle that we cannot overcome, no peril that we cannot face. But if we do not see to it that such ideas are propagated and accepted among people in their formative years, we cannot expect to find many who will be willing to cooperate. No matter how basically good the fruit trees in our orchard are, they will not blossom and bear fruit unless they are consistently well tended.

Good Egg

Look at an egg from the outside. It appears to be wholesome and good. This may be so, but it is not until we break the shell that we find out whether it is really good or bad.

The same is true of many human beings today. It is not until their outer shell is pierced that we come to know the truth about them. Their bodies swaddled in elegant clothes, their ideas couched in eloquent words, they strike us as being fine creatures indeed. But under the finest veneer there can lurk an ugly, repulsive character. It is not until one gets close and has dealings with such a person that one discovers—particularly when there is a clash of interest—how uninspiring is the reality. Behind the gentlemanly facade lies a bundle of selfishness, cheapness, affectation, pride, prejudice, exploitativeness and arrogance. Challenge such a person's interests, and we see him in his true colours. No good egg he!

In the vast morass of conflict which exists in the world today, it often seems that it is the hypocrite who remains supreme, the one who manages to project himself as the "good egg" to the rest of the world.

But this state of affairs can never last. The time is fast approaching when man will be ushered into another world where all hypocrisy will fall away, and all power will rest, not in the hand of man, but of God.

Road Block

When a road is under repair, a notice bearing the words "Road Closed" is put up to warn unwary travellers. But this does not mean that the path to one's destination is irrevocably barred. There are always other highways and by-ways—it is just a question of looking around for them. Sometimes one can reach one's destination just as well by zig-zagging through narrow lanes and alley-ways. The only difference is that this takes somewhat longer, and one has to keep one's wits about one to negotiate narrower roadways and sharper turnings. But arrive one finally does.

Life's journey is very often like this. One would like to proceed by broad straight routes, moving fast and reaching one's goal in the most direct possible way. But, so often such roads are blocked, and achieving success begins to seem a very difficult matter. But for every major route which is blocked, there are always several minor roads which are open. It is just a question of having to go about things in a roundabout way. This is particularly true if you meet with an adversary and feel that you are unable to confront him head-on. It is then that you must find some indirect means of dealing with him. Often compromise or adjustment is the best solution.

When in one particular field there seems to be a discouraging lack of opportunities, one can certainly search for and find opportunities in some other field. When you fail to find a place for yourself in the front row, you can always make do with one in the rear, until a place up ahead finally falls vacant for you. When you cannot find people to extend a helping hand to you, press on fearlessly and strike out on your own. When you need things from people to help you on in life and no one seems ready to be generous, stop thinking of how deprived you are and try instead to earn God's blessings.

For every closed door, there is always another which is open—but only to those who have the eyes to see it, and the courage to march through it.

Unlocking the Gates to Success

The guest struggled desperately to open the lock, and as he went on and on twisting and twisting and turning the key, and trying to jerk the lock open, his vexation finally turned to fury. "This lock is defective!" he shouted to anyone who cared to listen. Then he muttered under his breath that his host had been a fool to buy such a lock. The next to have his wrath vented on it was the lock-making industry, which produced worthless goods, not caring whether they worked or not and not caring whether people were put to trouble or not. Their business was only to make money out of unsuspecting consumers! By this time he was at the end of his tether and had decided he was going to break it open with a hammer. Just then, his host arrived and tried the key in the lock himself. "Oh, I'm so sorry!" he exclaimed." I quite forgot I had changed this lock, but I just momentarily forgot, and gave you the wrong key." He then produced the right key and the lock opened instantly. So the guest's ire had been quite misdirected and he had ultimately achieved nothing by it except reduce himself to a state of utter exhaustion.

How many latter-day Muslims find themselves in this sorry predicament, faced as they are with one impasse after another, finding areas which they urgently need to enter, difficult of access, nay, impenetrable, because the way is barred by locks to which they have the wrong keys. This modern age has changed the locks to life's doors, but we still carry the same old keys around with us, hopefully fitting them here and there, staring in incomprehension when locks do not snap open for us, and then frittering away our energies in senseless rage. We curse first of all the lock-makers, then the environment. But it is all to no avail, because you just cannot unlock new locks with old keys.

Our leaders, in their frustration, have thought fit to identify certain "enemies of Islam" and to trace all their woes to them—as if they were the sole purveyors of these impregnable locks. But in this world of God, there is no attitude more insensate than this. Here, if we feel deprived and thwarted, it is because we are already suffering the punishments for our own negligence and shortcomings. In this world, most of our afflictions are due to our failure to live up to the standard of the times. The day we realize how much we are out of step with modernity, we shall be in a position to remove all obstacles from our path. We must fit the right keys to the locks on life's gates, and all avenues will open before us.

Working Together

In the days of the steam engine, the engine drivers had no option but to stand at close quarters to a blazing fire. It was all part of being an engine driver, and without that no train could have run. Much the same thing happens to the individuals who make things go in civic life. They are confronted by the blazing fire of their own anger at other members of society.

They rage at wrongdoers, cheats and shirkers, both real and imagined. But just as the engine driver controls both the fire which drives the engine and his own desire to escape from it, so mustb the individual in society tame both his own fury and a desire simply to run away from adverse situations. If a society is to hold together and function in harmony, individuals must learn to bear with those who oppose and hurt them. There is no group of people in which differences of opinion do not arise;

no group in which there are never feelings of grievance and resentment. It would, indeed, be unrealistic to expect that everything should be plain sailing.

How then can people live and work together? How, with seemingly irreconcilable differences between individuals, can society be welded into a cohesive whole? There is only one way: people must bury their differences and agree to disagree. But this can happen only if people react coolly and rationally in difficult situations where relations are strained and there seems no way out of the dilemma. It can happen only if people are fully aware of their responsibilities towards others, as individuals, and towards their community as a whole.

This may seem to be asking the impossible. But this is not so. Every individual does these things in the most natural way within his own domestic circle. In quite normal families, differences of opinion occur almost every day, but the bonds of love and kinship prevail and grievances are all finally buried. It is in this way that a family holds together. Every home is a practical example of people agreeing to disagree.

This spirit of give and take which is a matter of instrict in a family, is something which can emerge in a community only through conscious effort on the part of its members. While it is an emotional bond that keeps families from disintegrating, it is a rational effort which cements society, constraining its members to hold together despite all differences.

In the Nick of Time

A medical college professor, putting a student through an oral examination, asked him, "How many of these pills would you give to a man who had suffered a heart attack?" "Four," replied the student. A minute later, he piped up, "Professor, can I change my answer?" "You can, by all means," said the professor, looking at his watch. "But, regrettably, your patient has already been dead for 40 seconds."

Certain matters in life are so critical that they require the appropriate step to be taken without a moment's hesitation. But an instant decision must also be a correct one, otherwise the consequences could be drastic, and could mean a lifetime of repentance.

Our moments of decision-making are often very similar to our attempts to board a train. Catching a train requires preparation. We have to pack up our luggage, making sure we take the right things with us, buy a ticket, arrange transport to take us to the station and we must, of course already be on the platform at the appointed time, otherwise we are surely going to be left behind. For the train is no respecter of persons. It arrives on time and departs on time, and pays no heed whatsoever to tardy passengers. If we are like the medical student who was caught on the wrong foot because of lack of preparation and who was much too late with the correct answer, the train of life will go on its scheduled course and we shall be left standing, wondering what to do next and how to avert the disastrous consequences of our failure to get on board. It is, therefore, necessary to be prepared for all eventualities in life. That means assiduously acquiring a good education and losing no time in gaining useful experience relevant to our chosen occupations. It above all requires a mental and physical readiness to seize opportunities when they come our way, and to be firm of purpose, never permitting one's energy to be frittered away in pointless vacillation. (116:2)

The Human Personality

If from a vessel containing water a single drop is found to be brackish, it means that all of the liquid is undrinkable. We need sample only one drop to know with certainty what the rest will be like. Much the same is true of the human personality. It is like an overbrimming vessel which keeps on shedding drops for other people to savour, to find sweet or brackish as the case may be. Small instances of an individual's behaviour and quite short interludes in his company are generally sufficient to tell us what his overall personality is like—unless we are dealing with the greatest of dissemblers! A thoughtless remark, an unfair manoeuvre, a failure to give much-needed sympathy or support, a devious transaction—all these are the plain indicators, like those brackish drops of water from the larger vessel, which indicate the lack of integrity or callousness of the person you are dealing with.

The human personality has the same homogeneity as water. A single human weakness cannot therefore be considered in isolation, as if it were an exception. It has to be looked upon as being representative of the entire personality. If an individual proves unreliable in one matter, he is likely to evince the same unreliability in other matters; if he is guilty of untrustworthiness on one occasion, the chances are that this trait will show up time and time again.

There is only one kind of person who is an exception to that rule, and that is the one who subjects his own behaviour to constant re-appraisal, who is continually scrutinizing himself for weaknesses and faults and who, once having found such faults, wastes no time in rooting them out.

A man who has made a mistake can completely erase the marks of what is an unfortunate experience for others by admitting his mistake and begging forgiveness. Some people are pricked by their consciences, but do nothing to assuage the ruffled feelings of others, thinking that to do so would be sheer weakness and would mean a loss of face. Such people can never have healthy social relationships and can never win the respect of their fellow men. They do not realize that a man displays his true mettle when he sees his own wrong actions for what they are, and humbly asks forgiveness.

It is only he who has learned the art of moral intropsection who will, in the long run, prove himself a person of inviolable integrity.

Concentration

Charles Darwin (1809-1882) one of most famous thinkers of modern times, (although the writer does not agree with his views) played a major part in the intellectual formation of modern man.

Darwin achieved this position of eminence in the modern world by dint of exceptionally hard work. *The Encyclopaedia Britannica* (1984) says of him:

"All his mental energy was focussed on his subject and that was why poetry, pictures and music ceased in his mature life to afford him the pleasure that they had given him in his earlier days." (5/495).

Such intellectual concentration is vital to peak achievement in any field, be it right or wrong. Man has to be so engrossed in his work that everything else pales into insignificance beside it. Unless everything else loses its interest for him, he cannot climb to any great heights of success. If we examine the lives of the truly great, we find that they all worked in the same dedicated way.

In any task of greater or lesser complexity, there are always aspects of it which present problems which appear at first sight to be insoluble. Sometimes innumerable facts have to be marshalled which can be interpreted only with the keenest of insight. Often a mysterious, elusive factor emerges just at a point when one thinks that all questions have been answered. Such difficulties can be overcome, and such secrets unveiled only when one's total intellectual capacity is directed towards the unraveling of the mystery. Without the utmost devotion and one hundred per cent concentration, success will remain forever beyond one's grasp (125:20).

A Shaft of Light

The owner of a transport business once found himself in weak and vulnerable position because, for technical reasons, he had once had one of his vehicles registered in the name of another person several years before, and that person still held its licence. The licence-holder decided one fine day that he would take possession of the vehicle himself, and that its real owner would have to make do with a paltry sum of money in exchange. The owner naturally felt that the most dreadful injustice was being done to him and, greatly incensed, he was determined to have his revenge. Night and day he lived in a frenzy, thinking of ways and means to eliminate his enemy. Truly he wished to crush him like an insect. For six long months he lived in this state of morbid preoccupation, losing all interest in his home and his business, and becoming, finally, like the ghost of his former self. Then, one day, he had an experience which changed the course of his life. As he was pacing up and down one of the streets of the town where he lived, lost in black, vengeful fantasies, he heard the unmistakable sounds of someone making a speech before a large gathering. Curious, and for once drawn out of himself, he approached the gathering of people and began to listen to the speaker. He was suddenly struck by what he was saying: "Think well before taking revenge, for you too shall suffer the vengeance of others." It was as if a shaft of bright light had suddenly penetrated his mind and with each example that the speaker gave to drive home his point, he felt himself turn into a new person. He decided there and then to give up his negative way of thinking, in fact, to forget the whole sorry episode, and to devote his time and energy to his family and his business. The full realization had come to him that it was on himself that he had inflicted suffering and not on his enemy, and that it was best to leave such matters to God. In beginning to think in this way, he found that; bit by bit, he was once again able to make a constructive approach to things and it was not long before he became more successful than he had ever been. In pursuing positive ends he had also attained peace of mind, and that, for him, had been the most important thing of all.

Narrow-Mindedness

According to La Rochefoucauld: "Mediocre spirits generally condemn everything that exceeds their small stature." Perceiving this common human failing, a modern poet implores people: "Don't criticize what you can't understand."

The trouble is, people tend to judge matters on how they affect their own selves. They are quick to support anything which improves their own position, or at least does not downgrade them in any way. But when something appears threatening to their own position, they oppose it, regardless of its intrinsic worth.

Take, for example, the case of our Arabic madrasahs (schools) functioning in the Indian sub-continent. Generally, they include a course in ancient Aristotelian logic in their syllabus. We say "logic," or that is the name by which this science is known, but it would be more accurate to call it "illogic". What is taught in the name of logic has nothing to do with true logic. It is not conducive to the logical presentation of Islam vis à' vis modern education.

The administrative authorities of one such Arabic school decided unanimously to withdraw all text-books on classical logic from their syllabus. A new course in philosophy was to be prepared, conforming to modern academic standards. Unfortunately, however, they were unable to implement this decision. Why? Because the professor of logic in their institution opposed it tooth and nail. As he was a senior teacher in the school, the administrators were unable to go against his wishes.

One does not have to look far to see the reason for this opposition. This professor only had a knowledge of classical logic; he had no knowledge of modern philosophy. He feared that if classical logic were taken out of the syllabus, he himself would lose his status in the institution. He would be left like a teacher who knew only French, trying to get his point across in a school where the medium of instruction was Arabic. In this case, it was very small-minded of him to allow his own feelings of professional insecurity to stand in the way of modernization.

Another Day! How Wonderful

"When you wake up in the morning, jump out of bed and shout, 'Great! Another Day!' you are success." This was a view expressed by a prominent businessman, but it could very well be the scholar, the sage, the ascetic, depending upon how you interpret success. Anyone, in fact, who regards the new day with such potimism is surely well-equipped, mentally and emotionally, to tackle whatever life has in store for him. But, whether we regard the appearance of the new day as one more joyful occasion for work or not, can we honestly say that we have ever stopped to ponder over the miraculous aspect of day following night, for all eternity, as a result of the earth rotating on its axis and of the sun's never ceasing to flood with life-giving light our ever-changing hemisphere? Have we ever thought of this alternation of day and night as a totally unique occurrence, and of this all being part of the divine pattern which produces such advantageous conditions for human existence? Nowhere in the universe, in fact, are there prime conditions such as we have on earth for the emergence and development of life as we know it. Other heavenly bodies are either too hot, too cold, too gaseous, too windswept or too fiery, or can be like Jupiter and the moon, proceeding in their respective orbits without rotating on their axes, so that one half of the globe is permanently illuminated while the other is for ever plunged in darkness. The denizen of such a sphere would have no rising sun to stir his enthusiasm and no peaceful sunset to signal the moment for rest. He would have no periods of vigour and achievement alternating with soothing periods of repose. For the human being, accustomed to his diurnal-noctunal alternation, such an existence would be one of utter staleness and weariness, with no refreshment ever in sight. Yet this pattern, to which all living things on earth have been attuned from time immemorial, is something which we take for granted, and for which we do not consider it necessary to offer up our thanks. But this unique ordering of day and night is God's own doing, for the especial benefit of man, and we would do well never to lose sight of what an extraordinary blessing it is. (116:15)

When One is Broken in Two

When an inanimate object, such as a piece of wood, is broken in two, it remains broken. Never again can it remold itself into one piece. Animate objects, however, live on even after breakages. When one live amoeba is cut in two, it turns into two live amoebae.

This is surely a sign from God, showing us the wealth of opportunity that God has kept in store for us live human beings in this world. For a human being, no defeat is final, no disaster permanently crippling. As an animate being, no human can be finally shattered for, when broken, its every piece is welded again into a new, live being, if anything, more formidable than before.

For a human being, failure is not failure at all, for it only serves to make one into a more profound, thoughtful person. Obstacles present no hindrance, for they open up new avenues of intellectual advance. Setbacks do not stunt one's growth, for even if one is crushed into many small pieces, each piece in its own right has the capacity to form the building blocks of an entirely new being.

Such are the never-ending possibilities which God has created for man in this world, but it is only one who is alive to these possibilities who can benefit from them, gathering and marshalling his resources after some shattering setback. When he tastes defeat, he does not lose heart, but prepares himself to issue a new challenge. He builds anew his shipwrecked boat, and, aboard it, sets out once again on his voyage through life (118:9).

Destined for Great Deeds

One always finds two types of people in the world. On the one hand, there are those who want immediate reward for all that they do, with their recompense exceeding the work they have put in. Then there are those who are not out for any material reward. The knowledge that they have contributed in some way to a worthwhile cause is sufficient reward for them. If they receive no recompense for their efforts, it does not cause them concern or arouse their anger. They play their part, it does not adversely affect their personal contribution, so engrossed are they in the cause for which they are working.

Outwardly, both groups appear the same, but in reality there is a world of difference between the two. Besides their superficial similarity, the two have nothing in common. The first group, one might say, keep the markets of the world turning over, while the second group turn over new pages in human history. Such is the extent to which the two differ.

It is the second group who make meaningful, valuable contributions to the betterment of humanity, for it is they who are able to join in a common struggle, without which no worthwhile work can be achieved in this world. Whenever a number of people work together for a common goal, it is inevitable that some should receive more credit than others. Some are hailed for their achievements, while others are denied all recognition. This is true of all movements, whether popular or prophetic in nature. There is only one way for a common effort to prosper, and that is by people forgetting about their rights, and remembering only their responsibilities.

Unless there is a spirit of selfless struggle among those participating in a common cause, it is not only those who receive no recompense who will feel ill-treated. Even those who are rewarded for their contribution will feel that they have not been done justice. Seldom does the reward a person receives for his efforts live up to his expectations. It is a case of either being satisfied with nothing, or never being satisfied at all.

Those who are destined to perform great deeds in life are those who do not seek any reward for what they have done; the very fact that they have done something is sufficient reward for them. The knowledge that they have played their part is enough to make them content, even more so than those who have been abundantly rewarded for their efforts.

In Giving We Receive

According to *Time* Magazine of October 17, 1986, her Majesty Queen Elizabeth II had long voiced a desire to visit the People's Republic of China. But as long as Britain ruled a piece of Chinese territory, the crown colony of Hong Kong, such a journey was impossible. The 1984 Sino-British agreement returning Hong Kong to China in 1997 provided the price of admission (p. 22).

Returning Hong Kong to the mainland was no easy task, for it amounted to losing a jewel from the British Crown, but it was clear that the British Monarch's desire to visit China was not unconnected with Britain's avidity for trade with that country and, obviously, the ensuing gains would be immense. Relations between Britain and China had been uneasy over the last hundred years, but with the Queen's historic visit—the first ever made to China by a member of a British Royal family—the gates to trade were thrown open. A successful piece of diplomacy, it paved the way to an annual trade agreement of over one and a half billion dollars.

A jewel may have been lost from the crown, but the subsequent benefits will be enormous. Clearly, we have to give in order to take. That is the way of the world.

How Do You Win the Nobel Prize?

Nobel Laureate Professor Abdus Salam toured several Indian cities in 1986, and in one of the speeches he made (*The Times of India*, 16 January, 1986), he cited South Korea as an example of extraordinarily rapid national development. He said that about 15 years ago, the gross national product per capita there was equal to that of India, but that thanks to the efforts the Koreans had made, it was now many times more. Giving the example of the team who had come from South Korea to Trieste, in Italy, where he resides, to find out from him how Nobel Prizes were won, he said that a similar spirit needed to be inculcated in the people of the Third World. He felt that it was this questing spirit which was the basis for all progress, be it of an individual or of a nation, and that this was true of progress both in this world and in the world hereafter.

All too often a process of stagnation sets in in the affairs of a nation. It would appear that an impasse had been reached. Instead of effort, there is inertia. When this stage is reached, a nation begins to tumble in disarray down the ladder of progress towards the lowermost rung and it is only the seekers, the strivers, who can pull it upwards from such an ignominious position and set it back on the path of progress. It is only the questing spirit which can put it right back up on the topmost rung of the ladder of progress.

Gerard of Cremona

Gerard, who was born in Cremona, Lombardy, in 1114, was a mediaeval scholar who translated the works of many major Greek and Arabic writers into Latin, there being a great body of scientific and philosophical literature in these languages which were well worth making available to all the known world at that time. In this sense, he performed the same service for his countrymen that Hunain Ibn Ishaaq had done for eastern Arabia. He went specially to Toledo, in Spain, to learn Arabic so that he could read the *Almagest* by Ptolemy, the Greek astronomer, geographer and mathematician who lived in the second century A.D. The *Almagest* was a vast computation of the astronomical knowledge of the ancients, and was accepted as authoritative up to the Middle Ages and the Renaissance. As such, this was one of Gerard's most significant translations. He was assisted in his task by two other scholars, one Christian and one Jewish. With this, and other such books, the gates of Greek and Arabic sciences were opened for the first time to the west. In the field of medicine, he translated books by Buqrat and Galen, almost all of the books by Hunain and Al-Kindi, Abul Qasim Zuhravi's book on surgery and many other books on the physical sciences, including the pamphlet on fossils which is attributed to Aristotle. Besides these, he rendered into Latin Avicenna's massive volume on law and many other books by Al-Kindi, Al-Farabi, Ishaaq and Sabit, etc.

Many other purveyors of knowledge were later to follow in Gerard's footsteps. In the words of Dr Maz Mirhaf, 'He was the founder of Arabism in the western world."

In 1187, in Toledo, Gerard fell ill, and felt himself that his end was near. He wondered to himself what would happen when he was gone. "These books in Arabic are so precious," he thought, "and who is going to translate them into western languages?" His reflections moved him profoundly and he was fired with new zeal and energy. In spite of his rapidly failing health, he then succeeded in translating the remainder of his valuable collection of books. Legend has it that in the space of one month before his death, he had completed the translations of no less than 80 books.

When one feels sufficiently inspired to perform a task, one undertakes it at all costs, even on one's death bed, and even when one's external circumstances are totally adverse. It is one's will and one's motivation to work which are of prime importance. Health and strength are secondary.

Trust is Golden

With just a few hundred rupees capital, a man from Delhi started a business. He used to buy scraps of cloth which he would sell from door to door. When his business had grown somewhat, he obtained permission to sit on the pavement in front of a shop and sell his merchandise there.

This freelance cloth-merchant built up a good deal of trust with his wholesaler, whom he impressed with his honesty and fairdealing. The wholesaler began to grant cloth on loan to the vendor, who always made an effort to settle his debt before the appointed date. This habit made him even more trustworthy in the eyes of the wholesaler, who granted him more and more cloth on loan. After just a few years, the wholesaler was giving this street-vendor Rs 150,000 worth of cloth on loan, an amount which he would not have given anybody else except on the basis of a considerable cash downpayment.

Clearly, such a large amount of cloth could not be accommodated on the street. The cloth-vendor now required a shop. He bought one, and continued to spiral, and before long he was among the leading cloth-merchants of the old city.

It is a mistake to think of money as the greatest asset in life. The greatest asset is trust. On the basis of trust one can buy anything. What one lacks in other departments he can make up for in trust. Trust is an invaluable asset which can buy even more than money.

But the way to establish trust is not by repeating how trustworthy one is. No, it is by acting in a trustworthy manner. The outside world is very severe in this regard. Unless one proves one's trustworthiness by impeccable actions, one cannot expect to receive the benefit of the doubt. Only if one consistently shows oneself worthy of trust over a long period, as the cloth vendor showed himself in his dealings with the wholesale merchant, will one be accorded trust in this world (117:7).

The Secret of Success

Eighty per cent of the information received by a human being from the outside world comes to him through his eyes-provided he keeps his eyes open. There is an abundance of oxygen in the air, but if it is to do him any good, he must assiduously breathe it in. If, however, we are to benefit from our environment, it means rather more than just depending upon our own spontaneous biological functioning. It means that we must have the will and ability to seize the opportunities given to us by God and to learn to grapple with whatever their built-in conditions may be. We cannot expect the world—of its own—to lay its gifts at our feet.

This concept is of the greatest importance in the

sphere of *Dawah* work. The spreading of the Islamic message is not something which is going to happen automatically, and, if it is to come about, it will depend upon our grasping whatever opportunities come our way. In modern times the greatest opportunity that has presented itself is the widespread freedom of belief enjoyed all over the world. (Only in a few communist countries are curbs placed upon religious activities). This freedom, however, carries with it a tacit proviso, i.e. that propagation of the faith must not take place by coercion, but by gentle persuasion. One reason for this is that so long as one does not use force, there will be no serious opposition to such activity. Perhaps a more important reason is that everyone should enjoy the same freedom of belief; the forcing of beliefs upon others is tantamount to encroaching upon that freedom, nay, destroying it. Failure to respect this condition means misusing the opportunity which presents itself; *Dawah* activity carried on in this way would eventually prove counter-productive. After such an abuse of another's privilege, there would be nothing to stand between us and God's punishment, for it is He who has provided us with this unique opportunity to bring other people within the fold. It is an opportunity to be seized, not wasted.

Missed opportunities spell ruin. That is the way of the world. And that is the will of God. (114:10-11)

At the Olympic Games held in Los Angeles in July-August 1984, about 62 Indian sportsmen participated. When the games were over and they returned to New Delhi on August 16, 1984, they received a chilly welcome, as they had failed to win a single medal, neither gold, silver nor bronze.

What was the reason for this failure? According to a report published in the *Times of India* (August 17, 1984), "Lack of scientific and systematic training was the main reason for India's poor showing. We did our best but that, unfortunately, was not good enough. The entrants began their training just three months beforehand."

What has been said about the Olympic Games applies to all walks of life.

In this world of competition it is necessary to enter the field fully prepared. If you enter it inadequately prepared, little else but failure will await you.

Your preparation should conform to two requirements: it should be organized and it should be consistent with the standards of the times. If it is not so, you will fail to make your mark and you will be unable to keep in step with modern developments.

Reading the Signs

With the increase of traffic in modern times, the danger of accidents has also increased. To obviate this danger, various forms of road signs have been erected for the guidance of motorists. One such sign reads: "Lane driving is safe driving." Keeping to one's lane is an effective safeguard against accidents, averting the danger of colliding with other motor-cars, and ensuring that one's journey does not end in disaster.

An article in a British motoring magazine by an expert on driving gives some indispensable rules of thumb for drivers. If one is speeding down a main road, for example, and suddenly a ball appears from a side road, one must realize that there is probably a child not far behind it. If one sees the ball, but fails to see the child, one cannot count oneself a good driver. The really good driver stops, not on account of the ball, but on account of the child that he sees with his mind's eye running behind the ball. It is the quickness of his imagination which saves the child from being run over.

The principles we are required to keep in mind while driving are the same as those we should keep in mind on our journey through life. If one wishes, one can learn from the "highway code" the principle that one should follow in the vaster arena of life.

Always confine your activities to your own sphere; if you infringe on the sphere of others, you are sure to clash with them: your progress will come to an abrupt halt. When certain signs appear on the horizon of society, try to make out what these signs imply. Do not just go by outward signs; try to reach the meaning behind them. If one just goes by what one sees and fails to see what lurks in the background, one will not advance in one's journey through life. Others, more far-seeing than oneself, will forge ahead, while one falls victim to dangers that could have been avoided, if one had read the signs properly (116:4).

Aiming Directly at the Target

The American writer, Charles Gafield, who has made a thorough, psychology study of peakachievement, says that "in a study of 90 leaders in business, politics, sports and arts, many spoke of 'false starts but never of 'failure'. Disappointment spawns greater resolve, growth or change. Moreover, no matter how rough things get, super-achievers always feel there are other avenues they can explore. They always have another idea to test."

Reader's Digest, October, 1986

The writer emphasizes the fact, however, that these high achievers are neither superhuman, charismatic nor even singularly talented. What they do have in common is an "uncanny knach for increasing the odds in their favour through simple techniques that almost anyone can cultivate." He delineates five major areas of concern. First and foremost, one must have a great sense of mission, and a strong desire to turn everything that comes one's way to good account. Secondly, one must be result-oriented, so that one is not just preoccupied with unceasing activities, but with a definite outcome of one's efforts. Thirdly, one has to take stock of whatever knowledge and skills one has and bring out whatever is latent and waiting to be used, so that it can be tuned up to a peak of perfection. Very often, it is not so much a question of adding to one's knowledge and skills as of developing what is already there—capacities of which we are sometimes barely aware. Frequently, it is one's initial sense of mission which taps these hidden resources.

Sometimes it is impossible to achieve distant goals without the aid of one's fellowmen, in which case, one has to develop the capacity to inspire the team spirit in others. Particularly in highly competitive situations, it is essential to be able to encourage other competent people to make a significant contribution to one's own performance.

But no one sails through life without bumping into obstacles and suffering a variety of setbacks. This is when one must beware of lapsing into passivity. Then one has to take oneself firmly in hand and decide to look upon such things not as great gulfs from which one will never emerge, but simply as hurdles which have to be surmounted if one is to finish the race. One's initial feeling of disappointment should quickly transform itself into a great determination to try harder, to alter one's approach, to seek different and better ways of achieving one's goal, and to channel one's emergies more effectively towards their ultimate target.

Teacher Tree

The tree-trunk forms one half of a tree and the roots the other half. Botanists tell us that there is just as much of a tree spread under the ground as there is standing above the ground. The top half of a tree can only stand erect and verdant above the ground when it is prepared to bury its other half beneath the ground. This is an example which trees show to mankind; a philosopher puts it this way:

> "Root downward, fruit upward, that is the divine protocol."

The rose comes to a perfect combination of colour, line and aroma atop a tall stem. Its perfection is achieved, however, because first a root went down into the homely matrix of the common earth. Those who till the soil or garden understand the analogy. Our interests have so centred on gathering the fruit that it has been easy to forget the cultivation of the root.

A tree stands above the ground, fixing its roots firmly beneath the ground. It grows from beneath, upwards into the air; it does not start at the top and grow downwards. The tree is our teacher, imparting to us the lesson of nature that if we seek to progress outwardly, we must first strengthen ourselves inwardly; we must begin from the base of our own selves before we can hope to build society anew.

Starting from Scratch

"*I* have reached my present position by climbing a ladder and not by coming up to it in a lift." This observation was made by a tailor who had started with nothing but his own two hands and the will to work, and who had become eminently successful in his line of business. "Making a good coat is not child's play. The whole process is so complicated that without detailed information as to how to proceed, long experience and a high degree of skill, it is almost impossible to accomplish. It is only after a lifetime of hard work that I have succeeded in running a prosperous shop in the city."

The tailor went on to explain how he had served his apprenticeship under the guidance of an expert tailor. Just learning the art of cutting and sewing had taken him five long years. When he opened his own little shop, he discovered that he had difficulty in giving his customers a good fitting. This was because during his apprenticeship he had never really grasped the fact that people could be of such different shapes and sizes. He therefore set himself to the task of studying human anatomy, but it was only after many years of effort that he could make a coat with an absolutely perfect fitting. He eventually became so expert in this that he could even give perfect fittings to those who unfortunately suffered from deformities—such as hunchbacks. "In any type of work, there are many things which one has to learn on one's own. Often one cannot foresee these things at the outset, and each obstacle has to be overcome by hard work and ingenuity."

The tailor talked of many things of this nature concerning his skills, and it seemed to me as though I were listening to a lecture on the building of the nation by some very experienced person.

In truth, the only way to solve our economic and social problems is to follow the example of the tailor. After this initial apprenticeship, he had gone ahead and done things on his own. He had gone up by the stairs and not by the lift. There are no buttons which you can just push and then automatically reach your goals. You can only make progress step by step. Progress can seldom be made by leaps and bounds. By means of the ladder you can progress even to the stage of owning the lift, but you cannot make a success of your life by starting with the lift and expecting it to do everything for you.

Admitting One's Faults

A young player who had participated in a big football match for the first time, wrote to his father after his team had been defeated:

> "Our opponents discovered a great gap in our defence line, and that was me."

Such acceptance of one's shortcomings is rare, for it requires great courage. Without it, we cannot make social progress. Since every defeat is attributable to a gap in the line of defence, the best remedy is to accept it, for in so doing, one is well on the way to solving the problem.

No End to Possibilities

The sun was setting in the west over the mountains. Half of the orb had already dipped beneath the ridge. In a few minutes, the whole sun disappeared behind the still-glowing mountain range.

Then darkness began to set in on all sides. The light of the sun was gradually receding, and it seemed as if the whole area would be plunged in pitch darkness. But just then, another light began to ascend. It was the full moon, ascending in the east as the sun set in the west. In a short while the whole scene was lit up again. Not long after the eclipse of the sunlight, the earth was illuminated anew.

"This is a sign of nature," I thought to myself. "When one possibility ends, another begins. When the sun set, the moon came to give light to the world."

So, for individuals and nations, there is always

hope. If once one falls a victim to the hand of fate, there is no need to be discouraged. There is no cause for despair in this world of God. By grasping fresh opportunities and utilizing them one can arise again. All one has to do is go about one's task in an intelligent manner, and never give up trying.

God has created this world full of wonderful opportunities. Here, when matter perishes, it becomes energy; when darkness comes, a new light emerges from its depths; when one building falls, it leaves a place for another construction. So it is with events in the life of man. From every failure emerges the chance of new success. The same applies to rival nations. If one nation becomes advanced, while another remains backward, this is not the end of the matter. When this happens, another process begins: the advanced nations develop a love of comfort and luxurious living, which is likely, in the long run, to bring about its decadence and downfall while a new spirit of struggle and endeavour rises in the backward people to lead them on to greater heights.

This means that no one need lose heart in this world of God. However uncompromising circumstances may seem, they contain, somewhere or another, the possibility of triumph for man. What one should do is seek out this possibility, and use it to turn one's defeat into victory. Just remember that every dark cloud has a silver lining.

Perseverance

The following story, written by Mao Tse Tung, former Chairman of the Chinese Communist Party, is one which should set us all thinking.

In olden times, there was once an old man from the northern part of China who lived on the side of a mountain range which always lay in shadow. The problem was that there were two high mountains in front of his door which prevented the sun from entering his house. One day, the old man called to his young sons and said to them, "Let us go and remove these mountains by digging, so that the sun's rays may fall upon our house unhindered." A neighbour of the old man's, hearing of this plan, made fun of it. He said to the old man, "I knew that you were foolish, but I never realized that there was just no limit to your foolishness. How on earth is it possible to remove these high mountains just by digging them?"

The old man replied in all seriousness, "Yes, you are right. But when I die, my sons will dig, and after their death, their sons will dig. The digging process will thus continue for generations. The mountains, as you know, will not go on increasing in size, whereas each digging is bound to reduce them in size and, in this way, there will come a time when we shall have finally succeeded in removing these obstacles." The power to solve problems is always more significant than the problems themselves, and while problems are invariably limited, their solution is unlimited, there always being a number of different approaches which naturally vary, in scale and complexity. This story is a beautiful illustration of how a major feat necessitates not only long-term planning, but the willingness and determination to carry that planning into effect.

For a people who have the fortitude, to carry on their schemes from one generation to the next, working consistently and steadfastly, there is no mountain or river on earth which they will not be able to conquer.

Working in Unison

U.S. shipbuilders take sixteen months to complete a 50 thousand ton tanker. The Spaniards take even longer to produce a ship of similar tonnage—24 months. But Japanese shipbuilders do the job in just eight months.

What is the secret of this Japanese miracle? A survey conducted by western experts shows that the deciding factor is teamwork. Japanese workers and management function together in complete unison. At no stage during the work processes is this bond disrupted. The result is the production of high quality goods within an amazingly short time.

Group harmony is something which is part of the whole fabric of Japanese culture and work methods. Whether in the home or in the factory, in large institutions or small, the will to be cooperative manifests itself as the truly distinctive feature of the Japanese character. William Ouchi, an expert in Japanology writes : "Every activity in Japan is group activity and not a springboard to individual glory and personal advertisement." (*The Hindustan Times*, February 16, 1986)

It is to this speciality that Japan's greatest secret of national progress can be traced. The willingness of large numbers of people to work together with good grace is a prerequisite for success in any venture. The only flaw in this system of joint effort is that the personality of the individual has little opportunity to flourish. But it is only a nation which is made up of individuals who are prepared to make this personal sacrifice which can ever aspire to success. Where individuals keep pulling in opposite directions, no substantial progress can even be made at the national level.

When work is cooperative in spirit, well co-ordinated in organization and blessed with an atmosphere of harmony, the sky is the limit in quality and quantity of production. It is unity then which is the true key to success.

Unforeseen Circumstances

A woman belonging to Lima in South America, having failed to find a satisfactory job made up her mind to try her luck in North America, an affluent country. Too poor to afford an air fare, she conceived the notion of shutting herself inside a suitcase and having herself despatched as a piece of luggage. The plan was carried out.

The plane which carried her landed at the Los Angeles International airport. All the bags of the passengers were unloaded from the aeroplane for collection. All but one suitcase was uncollected. The police, therefore, intervened to open this abandoned suitcase and take into custody the goods inside, so that it could be handed over to the claimant whenever he turned up. Much to their horror, they unlocked it to find the corpse of a woman. Detectives were called in to investigate the case. They said:

"The woman may have been crushed by the weight of other luggage" (UPI).

This incident serves to illustrate one of life's truths: taking whatever steps we feel are necessary does not, in itself, ensure our success. This is because there are so many external and unforeseen factors involved which determine the course of our actions. We must take them into account whenever we are deciding upon a course of action. It is only when these factors are in consonance with the steps taken, that we can hope to reach our destination.

This state of affairs takes a more critical turn when the offender is a leader and he goes wrong in framing a policy which involves the whole nation. This is bound to cause widespread misery, if not total destruction. It is, therefore, imperative that a leader be as discreet and careful as possible in his decision-making. He should consider all of the possible pros and cons. He should look before he leaps. His failing to do so would amount to an unpardonable offence. It would be far better for him to take no action at all than to plunge the whole nation into strife and torment.

Capability and Alertness

Raja Mohinder Pratap (1886-1979) was one of those Indians who went to Russia and met Vladimir Lenin (1870-1924). He was one of a delegation of freedom-fighters who met the Russian leader in 1919. He tells how, when he entered the room of the first ruler of communist Russia, Lenin rose to his feet, and went himself to fetch a small armchair from the corner of the room. Raja Mohinder Pratap took his seat on the armchair and Lenin sat next to him on a sofa. The revolutionary leader's first sentence was:

"In which language should I speak: English, German, French or Russian?"

It was finally settled that the conversation would be conducted in English. Raja Mohinder Pratap offered Lenin a copy of his book 'The Religion of Love'. "I have read this book, " Lenin said, as soon as he took hold of it. Raja Mohinder Pratap was astonished. Where on earth could Lenin have obtained the book? The previous evening, Lenin explained, when Raja Mohinder Pratap had met his secretary to fix the time of appointment, he had given the secretary a copy of the book. "I took it from him and read it during the night, in order to familiarize myself with the thought of the person I was going to meet the next day."

Lenin was the founder of modern Russia. He was an extraordinarily gifted man. Two of his qualities—capability and alertness—are illustrated in the above incident. He had studied so assiduously that he knew four different languages and was able to converse fluently in each one of them. Then so alert and on-the-ball was he that—despite his enormous preoccupation with affairs of state—he read the book of an unknown Indian at night, just so that he could have some prior knowledge of that person's thought when he met him the next day. Lenin made every effort to cultivate this natural talent; he made the most of the opportunities that were provided him; that was how he rose to the ranks of triumphant world leaders.

These two qualities—capability and alertness—are required for any kind of work. They are indispensable for the service of the Islamic cause, just as they are essential to one working in some other, secular field.

Firstly one must be fully equipped with contemporary knowledge, and secondly one must show oneself to be absolutely prepared in whatever one does. Lenin showed how one, equipped with these qualities, can achieve success in the secular field. If people who show capability and alertness of this nature apply themselves to the service of the Islamic cause, then they too will achieve the desired goal.

Talking Tall

A group of sightseers around Delhi zoo in the winter of 1985, looked at various animals in turn then paused in admiration before a great rarity—a solitary white lion which was pacing up and down outside its den.

"This is the only white lion left in the whole world!" exclaimed a member of the group. "You see, the Maharajah of Rewa owned two white lions, both of which he handed over to the Indian government after independence. One of them died, and we are now looking at the one which was left—the sole survivor of its species!"

If this gentleman had cared to walk a little further, he would have seen a board attached to the white lion's cage on which the zoo authorities had given detailed information, namely, that 69 white lions still exist in the world today, 25 of which are to be found in India alone. Yet just a few yards away there was a gentleman who claimed that there was just one white lion left in the whole world, and that was the one in the Delhi zoo.

How ignorant people can be of established facts, and yet how keenly they feel the urge to expound their views as if there were nothing in the world that they did not know.

Before holding forth on a subject, one should make a thorough study of it, for opinions based on inadequate research are bound to mislead the unwary. Empty utterances may impress the ill-informed, but to the knowledgeable, intelligent listener, they are simply a proclamation of the speaker's ignorance.

Sadly it is often the greatest if ignoramuses who make the weightiest of pronouncements (111:18).

A Life-time of Devotion

For no less than forty years, Pandit Ashu Ram Arya, a Vedic scholar, has been busy completing his self-ordained mission to translate all of the four Vedas into Urdu.

He embarked upon his task when he was just 20 years old. Now he is in his 70th year.

Pandit Arya said in an interview that his life's mission would be completed next year when he finished the translation of Sam Veda in Urdu and publishes it. Then for the first time, the translation of all the four Vedas in Urdu would be available.

His translation of the Yajurveda in Urdu was published this year and his translations of the Rig Veda and the Atharva Veda are already being printed in New Delhi and Chandigarh.

Before him, several scholars have attempted to translate the Vedas into Urdu, but their efforts have taken them no further than putting the Hindi "Rig Veda Adi Bhashya Bhumika" (only the gist of the Vedas) into Urdu.

Right Man—Right Results

The late Sir C.V. Raman (1888—1970), who received the Nobel prize for physics in 1928, achieved international repute and is still the most famous name in the field of Indian science. His discovery, known as the Raman effect, is one of the established pieces of scientific information which is useful in the study of molecular energy levels.

Born in an ordinary family, (his father was a school teacher drawing a monthly salary of Rs. 10), Raman had to work hard in difficult circumstances to make his way to the top. This is how he described his journey to success—"A long history of frustration, disappointment, struggle and every kind of tribulation."

All great men have their detractors, and one of them, wishing to underrate his academic success, commented that his famous discovery had been a mere accident, as in the case of many other scientists who had discovered important things just by chance. On hearing this, Raman displayed no annoyance but replied quite seriously that "the idea that a scientific discovery can be made by accident, is ruled out by the fact that the 'accident' if it is one, never occurs except to the right man."

Dr Raman summed up the process of discovery in these words: "The right man, right thinking, right instruments and right results." (*The Hindustan Times*, January 17, 1987)

Man's True Purpose in Life

Man attains his highest distinction only when he leads a purposeful life. Such a life characterises the most advanced stage of human development. This does not mean that by taking up just any task which is apparently significant man's life becomes truly purposeful. A really purposeful life is one in which man discovers his supreme status; a life in which his personality makes manifest its unique distinctive quality. An animal strives to obtain food; a bird flies in search of a better country when the seasons change; a wasp busies itself building up its own home from tiny particles of earth; a herd of deer takes measures to protect itself from wild beasts of prey. All of these appear to be purposeful actions. But when the phrase 'a purposeful life' is applied to man, then it does not refer to efforts of this nature. Without doubt arranging for one's food, clothes and habitation are some of the tasks that man has to perform in this world; but this is a level of purposefulness in which men and animals, being concerned only with bare survival, are equal. Its true application in relation to man can only be one in which he appears in all his dignity. Man's life becomes purposeful only when it goes beyond common animalism and takes the form of superior humanism.

God's creations in this world fall into two categories: animate and inanimate. Obviously, animate objects enjoy a certain superiority over inanimate objects. The former can be divided into three classes: the vegetable, the animal and the human. Modern scientific research has shown that plants also possess life, in that they nourish themselves, they grow and they have feelings.

But animals and men surely represent a higher form of life. In what way does man excel animals? Many theories have been advanced in answer to this question over the ages, and great minds are still studying it. But modern biologists have come to the conclusion that it is man's capacity for conceptual thought which distinguishes him from other life-forms. Animals lack this quality, whereas man is conscious of the fact that he is thinking. He consciously forms a plan of action in his mind; in his everyday life his actions are determined by himself. Whereas this is not the case with animals. Though many of their actions appear to be like those of men, they are not the result of thought; they all stem from pure instinct. Animals are simply led intuitively by their desires and their needs in a certain direction. Their actions are governed by environmental stresses from without and physical pressures from within.

It is in terms of this unique conceptual quality of man that we can conceive of what his higher purpose in life should be. The latter can only be one which does not result from the pressures of desire or of immediate exigencies. It must emanate from his own urge to worship God.

Man's true purpose in life can only be one which reflects the higher side of his personality; one which displays him as the superior being he is.

If one pauses at this stage to take note of what the Qur'an has to say, one will find that it gives us clear guidance in this matter. Man's purpose in life has been explained in the Qur'an in the following words:

I created mankind and the jinn that they might worship me. I demand no livelihood of them, nor do I ask that they should feed me. God alone is the Munificent Giver, the Mighty One, the Invincible.

The Bigger the Better

In his book, *How to Stop Worrying and Start Living*, first published in 1948, Dale Carnegie mentions that when he started writing it, he offered a two hundred-dollar prize for the most helpful and inspiring true story on "How I Conquered Worry." A story written along these lines was sent in by a Mr C.R. Boston, one of the most significant parts of which we reproduce below:

"I lost my mother when I was nine years old, my father when I was twelve. We were haunted by the fear of being called orphans...Then Mr and Mrs Loftin took me to live with them on their farm. Mr loftin told me I could stay there 'as long as I wanted'...I started going to school. The other children picked on me and poked fun at my big nose and said I was dumb and called me an 'orphan'. I was hurt so badly that I wanted to fight them, but, Mr Loftin, the farmer who had taken me in, said to me: 'Always remember that it takes a bigger man to walk away from a fight than it does to stay and fight.'

What is meant here by 'bigger'? In this context it has nothing to do with being taller or stronger, but signifies greater-hearted, broader-minded, and more able than a 'smaller man' to sustain injury or insult without losing one's composure. One's 'bigness' here has to do not with physical hardihood, but with moral courage.

No Half Measures

A noted western writer once, after studying the lives of great men, attempted to pinpoint the special qualities that were common to all of them. He came to the conclusion that all of the men he had studied had been filled with curiosity and discontent. Curiosity had kept them in hot pursuit of things, ideas and ideals which had at first eluded them, and discontent had never allowed them to indulge in the thought that they had reached the final peak of achievement. These qualities had proved to be the mainspring of their inspiration.

A similar comment is made by Mrs Anita Straket, a mathematics adviser from Wiltshire, in a 108-page educational report she had compiled for the school's council. Evaluating certain traits in talented children, she says, "Pupils who are impatient with anything that is second best are probably gifted." (*The Hindustan Times*, 2 February, 1983).

A demanding temperament of this kind compels one to go on seeking absolute truth. It prevents one from being content with half-truths and paltry successes, and one is continually spurred on to higher and greater things. Such a temperament demands that duties should be carried out in an ideal way and, indeed, anyone so inclined can never know happiness unless and until things have been done in the best possible way. A man endowed with such a temperament will never stop until the highest good has been achieved. There can be no half measures for him and he will never be content with things of lesser value.

The Learner-Teacher

Having a mission in life is the greatest spur to achievement

Within a few days of landing in Bombay, in November 1922, a young Spanish priest by the name of Fr. Henry Heras found himself in the presence of the St. Xavier's College, Bombay. He met the principle of the college. The young priest was a historian, and had a degree in Spanish history. "Which branch would you like to teach?" the principal asked him. "Indian History," Fr. Heras replied. "What do you know about Indian history? the principal asked him. Fr. Heras said he knew nothing "How, then, are you going to teach it?" "I shall study it." Fr. Heras answered.

To those who knew that he had a degree in history from Spain, it might have seemed strange that he did not just choose a branch of the subject with which he was thoroughly familiar, then settle into a comfortable teaching routine which would bring him his salary with the minimum of effort. Strange indeed, until one discovered that his purpose in doing so was to bring him into contact with the widest possible range of young people in order that he might the more effectively pursue his mission. It was essential that he should have a permanent base from which to work, and this kind of teaching assignment was ideal in that it gave him the opportunity to function both intra—and extra—murally.

So intent was be upon carrying out his mission that he did not once baulk at the enormity of the task that lay ahead. It meant learning the history of a whole sub-continent—and one, too, which dated back to the most ancient of times, and into which were interwoven the histories of many peoples. The comlexity of the task was intersified by the lack of documentary evidence for certain important periods of Indian history and the fact that much had to be pieced together on the basis of archeological discoveries. But he set about his task with such thoroughness and determination that he became not only an accomplished teacher of history, but a historian of repute of the same class as Sir Jadunath Sarkar and Dr Surendra Nath Sen. He died in 1956, but his work is still commemorated by an institute in Bombay which is named after him: the Heras Institute.

It is when one has a great and over-riding mission in life that no task seems too difficult, no hardship too great. That is when temporary gain loses its attractiveness and loss seems of little importance. There are many Muslims in the world today who let it be known that they are 'interested' in doing missionary work.

But are they ready to make the enormous sacrifices and engage in the unremitting toil which true missionary work demands?

The Beginning of a New Era

With the end of the 14th century Hijrah, a whole era of Islam has come to an end. With the beginning of the 15th century we are now on the threshold of a new era-and one of great promise, for we are fortunate in having around us all the circumstances most conducive to the creation of a new and great era of Islam.

When the darkness of the night gives way to the light of the sun, it is nature's silent way of announcing that one revolution of night and day is over and that with a fresh day, a fresh life is beginning, and that with the light of day, the wayfarer may take courage and hope to reach his destination. The morning sun sheds light on two views of life. One backward looking, one forward, looking. One is of the opportunities left behind, while the other is of the opportunities still ahead, waiting to be seized. He who uses his opportunities well will surely be successful in life. In this world of trial and competition, however, opportunities appear as such only to those who are capable of availing of them. Fail to grasp them and you will find that opportunity seldom knocks twice. Success, in other words, means the immediate exploitation of existing opportunities.

No one can make his start from yesterday. If a start is to be made, it must be from now, today. Those who choose to live in the past can expect little other than a steady deterioration of their circumstances and final annihilation.

Forget lost opportunities and learn to make full use of the chances of today. Just remember that the day once gone is gone never to return, and you may expect no quarter to be given you by the relentless march of time. Strike while the iron is hot, and success will surely come your way.

Super Performers

A book published in America in 1986, entitled *Peak Performers*, makes a study of the lives of a number of individuals in modern America who have played a heroic role in life. One point which the writer especially emphasizes is that a great mission can beget in a man the powerful urge to superior effort which ultimately leads him to exceptional achievement.

America sent its first manned spacecraft to land on the moon in 1967. The launching of the rocket had been the result of the combined efforts of a large number of experts, who had been engaged to work for this mission. One of this team, a computer programmer, said that something extraordinary began to happen as the work got under way. The thousands of ordinary men and women, who had been working to make the space programme materialize, had all of a sudden been transformed into super-achievers. They had started performing with an efficiency that they had never in their whole lives been able to muster.

Within the short period of 18 months, all of the work had been accomplished with exceptional rapidity.

"Want to know why we're doing so well?" our manager asked me. He pointed to the pale moon barely visible in the eastern sky. "People have been dreaming about going there for thousands of years. And *we're* going to do it."

It is understandable that what inspires a man more than anything is to have a great mission before him. That is what arouses a man's hidden potential and makes him capable of all manner of sacrifices. It makes him, in short, a peak performer.

The Purpose of Life

These verses specify man's purpose in life as worship. This is a purpose which elicits from man his uniqueness in its ultimate form. It raises man to a much higher plane than that of animals. Not a trace of animalism contributes to the achievement of such a goal. God does not demand of you a livelihood, the verse states, rather He himself is responsible for your livelihood. This means that worship of God is a purpose which is motivated neither by inward desires nor outward influences. Rather it comes into being through thought alone. Only when a person goes beyond his self and his environment can he understand that there is a higher purpose on which he should focus his life.

The motive force towards the fulfillment of this purpose is not the urge to satisfy one's needs or those of others. The worshipper seeks neither to gratify his own desires nor those of the Being he worships. It is a purpose which sets before man a goal far above all these things—a goal which does not follow internal needs or external pressures, but results purely from conceptual thought.

When a person works, makes money, builds a house, makes an effort to improve his standard of living, he appears to be engaged in efforts towards some worthy end. But a life of this nature cannot be called a purposeful life, for these activities do not demonstrate man's unique status. It might seem as if they are the result of deliberation, but if one looks at the matter in depth, one will see that in actual fact the motive force behind these actions is the same urge that motivates an animal in various ways, in its concern for its own survival. It is the driving force of one's desires; the pressure of one's needs, and the wish to fulfill the demands of one's self that underlie such a life. These are the considerations which, in fact, guide a person in his search for his livelihood.

When man grows up, he realizes that there are certain material necessities without which he cannot live. He requires food, clothes, a place to live; he requires a reliable source of income to sustain him throughout his life. He is forced by these considerations to obtain these things. Then he sees that those who have an abundance of these material things enjoy respect and apparently possess every form of happiness and luxury in this world. Thus he is driven on to do more than just seek a livelihood; he desires to earn to a degree greatly in excess of his actual requirements.

In bustling markets, grandiose offices, and opulent buildings, he is not really guided by deliberate thought. Rather, he is being guided by inflated ideas of his own needs, desires, longings and ambitions to achieve fame and high status in this world. For this reason these activities cannot be considered as being directed towards the purpose which sets man apart from the animal and lends him a higher distinction.

Man's greater dignity can be based only on a purpose which emanates from inner desires and pressures of environment. Man's true purpose in life can only be to seek the pleasure of God. When man seeks the pleasure of his Lord, his human qualities find full manifestation. This is a purpose loftier than the one towards which an animal directs its energies. It distinguishes man from animals. It is the ultimate station of human dignity.

To determine the purpose of life is , in short, the effort to make life meaningful. It must surely, therefore, be one which is in accordance with man's unique status; it must be one which leads man on the path to success and progress in terms of his true nature.

Reciprocity

When a certain tyre company of the western world was on the point of launching its goods on the market, it ran an advertising campaign which promised that "whoever demonstrated a real defect in the tyres would win a prize of $ 50,000." People naturally flocked to buy them. If they found a defect, well and good. If not, they had nothing to lose, because they would actually have purchased a good set of tyres.

The company did then actually receive a number of complaints of which 20 percent appeared to be genuine. The complainants were duly sent invitations to a seminar, their travelling expenses to be paid for by the company. This gave them the opportunity to air their respective views as to how the tyres could be improved. A concrete proposal was finally arrived at by consensus and rewards were distributed at the closure of the seminar.

By taking into consideration the suggestions of its customers, the Company was able to improve upon the quality of the original tyre. Although the cost had to be increased considerably, the tyres sold far outnumbered previous sales. Formerly the tyres had been manufactured according to the company's own formula, while the improved version was based on the opinions and suggestions of the consumers as well. It was only natural that people should regard the product as being far superior to the original one.

In this world all people—not just manufacturers and consumers—are dependent upon one another. It is, therefore, only sharing and cooperation which can lead to success in this life. It is the principle of give-and-take which should be most active, like two-way traffic. A system of benefits can never be a one-way thing, Reciprocity should be the order of the day.

Through Fire and Water

As Dale Carnegie—that most pragmatic of modern thinkers—once remarked: "The most important thing in life is not to capitalize on your gains. Any fool can do that: the really important thing is to profit from your losses. That requires intelligences; and it makes the difference between a man of sense and a fool.

It is seldom in this world that aspirants to wealth and fame meet with nothing but success throughout their careers. Many are the trials and tribulations through which they must pass before they can savour the fruits of their endeavours. The people who ultimately succeed are those who are undaunted by disadvantageous circumstances, who waste no time in lamenting over them and who give their attention instead to over coming whatever difficulties they are faced with.

The idea of profiting from one's losses may seem paradoxical, but it is something definitely worth aiming at, whether it be an individual, a group or a nation whose welfare is at stake. It is not, after all, the man who has never had to face any difficulties whatsoever who is necessarily the most successful in life. The truly successful person is one who can carry his ambitions into effect no matter what hurdles he has to leap over. He is the one who will arrive at his destination no matter what obstacles are strewn in his path. He is the one who is prepared to battle through fire and water right to the very end.

Patience, Perseverance and Compassion

"Success is a matter of cool decisions, without constant wavering and changing of the mind, acute observation, initiative, and unremitting attention to a vast number of petty details."

The above statement would appear to be a sure-fire recipe for material success in a very large number of situations.

As it happens, it is a formula evolved from the experience of Campbell Rogers, an expert in poultry keeping of international repute. But this unswerving devotion to taxing minutiae is not all that he advocates. He begins his now famous book, *Profitable Poultry Keeping in India and the East* (D.B. Taraporevala Sons & Co., Bombay, 1959) with the notion that success in large-scale poultry-farming is largely dependent upon one's temperament. Just as the successful poultry-man must give his attention to the habits and requirements of his birds, so also must the social being taken into account the inclinations and compulsions of others and show his willingness to make concessions to them in the interests of maintaining the happiness and tranquillity of society. Success in life is not just a matter of keeping one's nose to the grindstone and taking correct decisions about financial matters, but of understanding one's fellow-men and according them the kindness and respect which one would wish to have oneself.

What Must Be Known Before One Can Understand

In 1970 a certain Indian politician went to France. There he met with a French politician who was associated with the ruling Gaullist party. An extract from their conversation appeared in *The Times of India*, July 18, 1983:

"Is there anything in particular you would like to do in Paris?" asked the Gaullist.

"I am a great admirer of de Gaulle," replied the Indian visitor. "I should like to make a courtesty call on him."

"But he is dead, sir."

"What? Nobody told me in India during the briefing."

They must have presumed you were aware of it. He died four years ago."

From this example we can see that everything cannot be spelt out in words; there are some things that one has to know oneself. If one already knows half, then one can be told the rest of the story; but if one does not have half of it in one's mind beforehand, then how can one grasp the whole picture? However reasonable a thing may be, and however well substantiated, if one does not have some prior knowledge of it, it will remain beyond one's comprehension.

If one says to someone, "So-and-so batsman scored a century," he will immediately understand that what is meant by a century is a hundred runs in cricket. But if one says, "A century of hard struggle is needed for the development of a nation," no one will truly understand; for no one can know what it is to devote oneself individually to constructive work for so long a period.

Disadvantage Turned to Advantage

Mahatma Gandhi was very shy by nature. In his book, *"My Experiments with Truth"*, he confesses that it was a long time before he managed to shake off his shyness. While studying in London, he joined a vegetarian society. At one of its meetings he was asked to make a speech. He stood up, but was unable to express himself. Finally he brought himself to voice a few words of thanks and sat down. On another occasion, when he was invited to express his ideas on vegetarian food, he set his thoughts down on paper, but was not even able to read out what he himself has written. Someone, however, taking pity on him, read his discourse for him.

After passing his examination in law from London, he started his practice in Bombay. Here again his shyness was a stumbling block. When he appeared before the judge in his first case, he was so nervous that he could not say anything. He had to tell his client that he would not be able to pursue his case, and that he should choose another lawyer for himself.

But, as Gandhiji writes, this apparent disadvantage turned to his advantage:

> "My hesitancy in speech, which was once an annoyance, is now a pleasure. Its greatest benefit has been that it has taught me the economy of words. I

have naturally formed the habit of restraining my thoughts. And I can now give myself a certificate that a thoughtless word hardly ever escaped my tongue or pen."

Mahatma Gandhi was well-known for his thoughtful and economical manner of speech. But this outstanding trait only came from another trait which few would consider outstanding. Initially his shyness prevented him from speaking in public; later on it made him thoughtful and economical when he spoke.

Reply without Reaction

Mr J. Krishnamurti, 90, is a well-known Indian thinker. When he is on a public stage, he folds his hands and says, "Sir, I am a nobody," or, "Sir, I am just a passer-by." Are we all nothing on reality? His answer is, "Yes, when you are as nothing, you are everything."

Islamic thinkers disapprove of thoughts of this kind for they lead to scepticism or monism, and both are just a philosophical license for irresponsibility and monism. Yet there is an example from Krishnamurti's life which can be quoted here with great pertinence.

Mr. J. Krishnamurti is fortunate enough to find a large audience at every speech he makes. Thousands attend his talks year after year, but he feels unhappy at their failure to move along with him. At the end of his discussions in Madras in February 1984, he asked the audience: "Will you change, sirs?" and declard, "You'll all go back and continue doing what you have been doing." For more than 50 years he has been travelling round the West and India, but has still not relaxed his efforts to make people see what he thinks ought to be seen.

Once a man in the audience asked him angrily, "Year after year you say that we are not going along with you; then why do you keep talking to us?" Mr Krishnamurti politely replied, "Sir, have you ever asked a rose why it blooms?"

When you are provoked by a remark of your critic, all you do is react. But when you resist provocation, you are able to give an answer which will render your critic speechless.

Finders, not Losers

One can sum up the state of the Muslim community today by saying that they are afflicted by a *persecution complex*. Wherever one looks, one finds Muslims haunted by a feeling of having lost something. Everywhere they are complaining of persecution by other nations, of having had something taken away from them.

Closer scrutiny will tell one the nature of those things that Muslims complain of having lost. One will find that it is political power, government posts, economic resources, social influence and material gain that Muslims feel they have been deprived of. To their mind, they have been done out of these things by other nations of the world.

But, in fact, the Muslims have only themselves to blame for the losses they have incurred. It is their own neglectfulness that has taken them where they are. It is not a question of their having been deprived; it is a question of they themselves having failed to come up to the required mark. Still, what is even more important is that, even along with all these losses, there is still one thing that no one can take away from them. They may have lost worldly wealth, but they are still possessors of great spiritual wealth. The religion of Islam is still with them, fully intact. They still have the final divine scripture, preserved in its original state. They are heirs of a Prophet whose teachings still retain the vitality of the days when he first imparted them to the world. What the Muslims have, then, is greater than what they have lost. How strange that they should feel their losses, mere trifles though they are, and be unaware of the much greater treasure that they still retain.

To say that the path to worldly progress is barred to the Muslims is a highly debatable point. But even if one goes along with the general consensus of Muslim opinion and admits that it is, then still they have the chance to excel in the next world, and success there is better and more lasting than worldly success. Why then should they be so concerned about worldly loss, when they still have access to the much greater gains available in the hereafter?

Muslims may not be able to find what they seek from men, but they can still find it with God. If they concentrate on serving the divine cause, then they will find that God will provide them, in much greater measure than men could ever do, with all that they seek.

Disunity: The Enemy's Weapon

*I*srael's former minister of defence, Moshe Dayan (1915-1981), wrote in his autobiography, *The Story of My Life*, "The Arabs, disunited and at odds with one another over every issue, big and small, present no threat."

1983 has seen the PLO disunited and at odds with one another. After their expulsion from Lebanon, a large proportion of Palestinians are dissatisfied with Yasir Arafat's leadership. They have united behind Abu Musa in their attempt to dislodge the veteran PLO leader. But Yasir Arafat is not willing to step down. Thus the Palestinians are split up into two groups and are fighting it out amongst themselves.

Reporting these events, *The Washington Post* has quoted this statement of the Israeli Foreign Minister, Yitzhak Shamir, "I must say that it is good for Israel that there are domestic quarrels, breakups and divisions within the organization of the PLO." In addition, *The Washington Post* has quoted an Israeli defence ministry official as saying that there is a belief in Israel that the increased intensity of the revolt against Mr Arafat in northern and eastern Lebanon has reduced the number of attacks against Israeli soldiers in the south last week. In the same vein, another official said, "They are busy among themselves, and that is good for us." (*Guardian Weekly*, July 3, 1983).

To fight with one's friends is to become one's own worst enemy. It is to destroy oneself as one's enemies are always seeking to do.

An Eye for a Talent

When the Industrial magnate, G.D. Birla (1894-1983), was thirty years old, he received a letter from an unknown student in Calcutta. This is what the student, in an informal and forthright manner, had written:

If only you can help me with an amount of Rs 22,000 for the purchase of a special type of instrument which has to be imported, I may assure you that I may be able to get the Nobel Prize for my discovery.

The effect of this appeal was immediate. Mr Birla replied to the student's letter at once, enclosing a cheque for Rs. 22,000. With this amount the student ordered the instrument he needed from abroad and carried on with his research. His estimate proved correct. When the results of his research came before the public, he won such acclaim that he was awarded the Nobel Prize for science.

This student was the very person who later became known to the world as Sir C.V. Raman. When he had won the Nobel Prize and been knighted, his brilliance was appreciated by one and all. But to appreciate his talent when he was just an ordinary student, when all his greatness was still hidden in the future, was an extremely difficult thing to do, yet G.D.Birla did it, and that is why his name is high on the list of the architects of modern India.

This quality displayed by Mr Birla, not only raises individuals to greatness; it also has a great part to play in the national uplift. If there are appreciative and sympathetic people like Birla in a nation, one can rest assured that the talent of its youth will not die out. Talented young people can hope to be provided with all they need to cultivate their latent potential. But if there is no one who appreciates talent in this way, then the only people to advance themselves in society will be those who happen to secure some high official position; and clearly no nation can have more than a few such positions to offer.

Labour of a Lifetime

Helen Hooven Santmyer is now 88 years old, crippled an half-blind. She also suffers from emphysema. Because of her infirmity, she resides permanently in a nursing-home in Xenia, Ohio, U.S.A.

Over fifty years ago, when Helen Hooven Santyer was working as a reference librarian, she started to write a book. At first she worked on it in her spare time. Then, when ill-health forced her to retire, she continued her work in the nursing-home where she now lives.

She wrote the whole book out herself, in longhand, on a ledger. In 1982, her work complete, she presented it to the Ohio State University Press for publication. The final manuscript filled 11 boxes. A handful of copies were printed, but the book met with no initial success. It seemed as if Helen Hooven Santmyer's name would vanish without trace from the American literary scene.

But at least one person who bought the book read it and liked it. He was praising it in an Ohio library one day when the librarian overheard his conversation. The word was passed on to a producer, then an agent, then the American Book-Club. Each party found the book entrancing and worthy of a greater audience.

Finally Helen Hooven Santmyer's book, entitled "...And Ladies of the Club," was nominated for the Book Club Award in January 1984. It won the Award, and with it a sum of over 1 million dollars.

Helen Hooven Santmyer did not seek fame or wealth from her novel. Its topic—the story of two Ohio families in the period between the American Civil War and the great depression of the early 1930's is obviously not aimed at the commercial market. The author believed that Sinclair Lewis had painted a false portrait of the American dream in his novel of the 1920's, "Main Street". She wanted to correct that picture. As Haynes Johnson writes in the Washington Post:

The author was clearly not in the market for big bucks. She obviously was motivated by saying something in which she believed. The bare account of how she produced the work over the years, in her spare time, in sickness and in health, in itself provides an astonishing testament of her perseverance. (*Guardian Weekly*, January 29, 1984)

Strong belief in something makes one rise above one's worldly situation. It makes one concentrate on one's end in life. No matter what hindrances and obstacles lie in one's path, one soldiers on until one reaches one's final destination.

The conviction that spurs a true believer on is faith in the life to come. He bears all forms of hardships, suffering and adversity in this world. He realizes that this emphemeral world is for the trial of man; in the next eternal world of God he will be rewarded for his efforts. As Helen Hooven Santmyer laboured for over half a century in the compilation of her book bearing all forms of adversity in her determination to attain her goal in life, so the believer labours all his life for the attainment of reward in the hereafter. And, as Helen Hooven

Santmyer's sustained effort bore her due reward in this world, so the believer's sustained effort will bear him due reward in the next world: he will be made to enter a paradise of eternal repose and bliss.

Quiet Endeavour

On December 17, 1903, the brothers Orville and Wilbur Wright became the first men to successfully pilot a heavier-than-air craft under both control and power.

Orville and Wilbur Wright were bicycle makers from Ohio. When they set out to construct a flying-machine, they started from the most primitive constructions, and persevered until they had developed a craft fit to usher in a new age for man. While engaged in their preparation, they maintained the utmost secrecy. In order to ensure privacy, they bought a 600 acre farm in Kitty Hawk, a remote spot in the North Carolina coast. They made no attempts to publicize their project. When the first flight was made, Harry P. Moore, marine reporter for the Norfolk Virginian Pilot, heard the news 55 minutes later from a guardsman at Kitty Hawk, Dan Simpson. He gave Moore the news that Orville Wright had been aloft for 12 seconds and had covered 120 feet.

This sensational news was received with scepticism by most national newspapers. When Moore sent out telegraph queries to newspapers all over the country, only five papers printed it. How could two unknown brothers, they thought, have achieved such a wondrous feat?

At the same time, much-publicized efforts to make the first flight in the history of man were continuing up the coast at Widewater, Virginia. The site was about thirty miles south of Washington D.C., the capital of America, and the eyes of the nation were on the project. The machine prepared there was the product of Samuel P. Langley, who was then America's most distinguished aeronautical scientist. Despite having the advantage of funds, publicity and expert know-how, attempts to make the first flight were unsuccessful. There were two failures, the last on December 10, 1903, before the Wright's epic feat.

The Wrights achieved by quiet endeavour what others could not achieve by much-publicized preparation. They kept their sights set firmly on the goal ahead of them, and ignored all other considerations. This is summed up in the response of Orville Wright to a question put to him after World War II, when terrible destruction had been unleashed by the airplanes that had been developed from his basic model. Had Wright thought that their invention would be used for such dreadful purposes as was now the case? "That day at Kitty Hawk," he replied, "we thought only of getting off the ground."

Overcoming Handicaps

A dancer from South India, Sudha Chandran, was only sixteen years old when she broke her right leg in an accident on May 2, 1981. She was immediately taken to a local hospital. Without taking the necessary preliminary precautions, such as cleaning her wound and administering anti-tetanus injections, the doctors put her leg in plaster from thigh to toe. As the pain increased, her parents shifted her to a hospital in Madras. When the plaster was stripped off, it transpired that her leg had begun to blacken—a clear indication that infection had reached the bone and gangrene had set in. The doctors did all that they could, but her leg could not be saved. On June 6, 1981, it was amputated three inches below the knee.

Sudha's unbounded love for dancing had not abated. "I want to dance," she used to cry in anguish. "Will I ever dance again?"

She was fitted with a modern artificial leg, known as the "Jaipur foot". The inventor of this foot, Dr P.K. Sethi, happened to meet Sudha's teacher, who told the doctor of his pupil's ardent and undying passion for dancing. The doctor replied: "Sudha will be able to dance like anyone with normal limbs. Only she shall have to be tough enough to put in the extra effort and bear initial pain."

When Sudha learnt of this, she immediately readied

herself for the initial pain. She resumed her pursuit in earnest, and by putting in extra effort, she once again perfected her performance. Her first post-accident appearance was in Bombay on April 1, 1984. Dance critics, who had seen her perform before the amputation, said that she was dancing better now than before, and that it was difficult to tell which leg was artificial.

One may be beset by the most grievous handicaps in life, but, it is always possible to rise above them, as Sudha Chandran did. However, one must be willing to endure some "initial pain"; and put in some "extra effort" to achieve one's goal.

The Virtues of Dependability

During a recent visit to Europe, Habib Bhai from Hyderabad purchased a camera from a shop at Lausanne in Switzerland, at a cost of about Indian rupees 5000. Before long he realized he had made a mistake. He could have bought it in Saudi Arabia much cheaper—for about Rs 3000, and he had been planning to visit Saudi Arabia on his way back to India. He decided to return the camera, but was at a loss to know what he should say to the shopkeeper. Still, he could not resist the idea of going to the shop and trying his luck. He went up to the saleswoman at the counter and asked her for a refund on the camera. Much to his astonishment, the lady did not even ask him why he wanted to return it. All she asked was: "Do you want the money in Indian or American currency?" She handed him a slip to take over to another counter where he would receive his money back. The money was immediately refunded as if it made no difference to the shopkeepers whether they had money or goods.

The reason that the camera was taken back without demur was that the shopkeepers were sure that before long another customer would come along and buy it. Their article was of dependable quality: If one person did not require it, another would.

The Japanese Experience

In August 1945, the U.S.A. dropped two atom bombs on Japan, thereby reducing two of its major cities to ruins. Strangely enough, the Japanese seem to bear no grudge against the Americans, for, they say, it had only reacted to Japan's violence in the arena of war. The responsibility, therefore, needs to be shared by each side. This realistic attitude on the part of the Japanese has seen them through all kinds of adversity and brought them to extraordinary heights of progress in modern times.

Both the big industrial cities, Hiroshima and Nagasaki, bustling with life, became enormous areas of devastation in a matter of minutes. Within a ten-mile radius every kind of life—human, animal and vegetable was blown to bits. One and half million people died on the spot. Ten thousand of them simply disappeared. Yet these cities have now been built up once again with wide streets, spacious houses, parks and gardens, all of which have a modern look. Only one ruined building has been left as it was, in order to remind one of the grim punishment meted out to the Japanese during the second world war.

When Mr Khushwant Singh visited Japan, he learnt, much to his astonishment, that the Japanese do not exploit the events of Hiroshima and Nagasaki, in order to discredit the U.S.A. It is other nations, on the contrary, who have exploited these events for this purpose. When Khushwant Singh asked the reason for this attitude, a Japanese replied in a surprisingly calm tone:

"We hit them first at Pearl Harbour. We killed a lot of them. They warned us of what they were going to do, but we thought they were only bluffing. They beat us fair and square. We were quits, and now we are friends (*The Hindustan Times* April 4, 1981).

A memorial has been erected to commemorate the dead, the victims of a gruesome tragedy. In the museum are displayed photographs depicting death and destruction on a mass scale. About 70 lakh Japanese visit Hiroshima every year to witness this spectacle. In the course of conversation with the Japanese, however, one can sense the hidden feelings of hatred against

Americans. But they do not let it rule their lives.

By virtue of such a temperament they have scaled such great heights of progress in a very short span of time. They own neither petrol resources nor mineral wealth, most of their raw materials having to be imported. Keeping all these drawbacks in view, it is most amazing that they have dominated world markets. This is mainly owing to the superior quality of their goods.

Mr Khushwant Singh also enquired about the prospects of the legal profession there. He was told that it was not a flourishing business, the reason being that the Japanese preferred settling disputes on their own to suing in the courts. Willingness to admit faults by each party is the surest way to bring quarrels to an end. It is only when either party seeks to place the whole blame on the other side, that the quarrel takes a turn for the worse. Whereas the very gesture of shouldering the blame softens up the other side, with the result that the dispute dies a natural death.

This realistic attitude has greatly benefited the Japanese in many respects. For instance, this makes if possible for them to place their trust in one another. They thus save the time and money they would otherwise expend on lengthy legal documents. There are fifty thousand lawyers in the U.S.A., while there are only 11 thousand in Japan. Such legal experts are just not in demand.

Most of the commercial institutions place their trust in verbal understandings. Formerly it was practised only among the Japanese, but now foreign investors have also started to take advantage of this practice. Avoidance of unnecessary legal obligations invariably speeds up the work.

Essentially, such an outlook gives rise to unity. It is undoubtedly the greatest force that contributes to the success of a nation. In the words of an expert on Japanese affairs the secret of Japan's success lies in "never quarrelling amongst themselves, always doing everything together," (*The Hindustan Times,* April, 1981).

The Law of Nature

Harry Emerson Fosdick has explained an important fact of life as follows:

> "No steam or gas ever drives anything until it is confined. No Niagara is ever turned into light and power until it is tunnelled. No life ever grows until it is focused, dedicated, disciplined." (*Living Under Tension*, by Harry Emerson Fosdick)

There is but one law of nature, which applies to both animate and inanimate objects. It is that there is a price to be paid for every end in life: without paying that price, nothing can be achieved.

In this world one has to sink before one can rise; one has to resign oneself to loss before one can gain, to backwardness before one can advance; one has to be able to accept defeat before one can claim victory.

The world in which man lives has been created by God, not by man himself. This may appear to be a simple fact, but it is one that man usually forgets in his everyday life. Since we are living in God's world, we have no alternative but to understand His laws, and follow them. There is no other way we can make a place for ourselves in the world.

Those who wish to advance and be successful in life without passing through the necessary stages, will have to build another world for themselves—one which satisfies their own requirements; for in the world that God has created, their dreams can never come true.

The Root Cause of Riots

What is the reason for the senseless manner in which Muslims react in the face of provocation? Perhaps we can trace it to their pride psychology. It comes into being when religion is no longer treated as a matter of responsibility, but as a matter of pride. Such an attitude towards religion plays a fair share in contributing to the degradation of the Ummat, the community of believers.

The Qur'an says: "The faithful servants of God are they who walk upon the earth modestly and, when the foolish ones address them, answer: Peace." (Al-Furqan, 63) However, the attitude is reversed when religious teachings cease to inspire people to do good deeds and a moral decline sets in. People then become proud and haughty. Whether or not they act upon the teachings of their religion, they believe that they continue to be the chosen people of God. Their attachment to their religion is reduced to lip service: it exists in theory but not in practice; in the outward form but not in spirit. When religion serves only to show one's superiority over others, a high degree of moral perversion has been reached.

People hold their heads high and declare that they are the upholders of a religion which has retained the pure and original form of monotheism. However, they contradict themselves by manifesting such reverence for personalities both alive and dead as should be accorded only to the Lord, their God. They take pride in saying that Islam teaches one complete equality, but they continue to discriminate between man and man. They are the first to pronounce in public that Islam exhorts one to do good and shun bad in all circumstances, but in private they disregard this. If their attention is drawn to this contradiction in their words deeds, they will turn hostile to anyone daring to criticize them.

They take immense pride in describing the sublime character of the Prophet, for instance, his resistance to provocation; yet they themselves become annoyed about quite trivial matters and even justify their negative attitude by asking why they should not react in the face of provocation.

Going Places on Home Ground

Paul Dirac, who died in November 1984, was known to the world as the developer of the mathematics of the quantum mechanical theory—in effect the physics of the smallest part of the atom. He received his initial education, however, not in the field of mathematics, but in that of electrical engineering. Though he obtained a first-class degree at the Merchant Venturers Technical College, he did not excel in this subject. As J.G.Crowther wrote in his obituary: "His teachers did not consider him a genius." (*The Muslim*, Islamabad, November 23, 1984).

It was only when he entered the mathematics department of Bristol University, and then went on to St. John's College to continue his studies in the same field, that "it was perceived that he had extraordinary intellectual powers."

In the field of mathematics, Dirac was on homeground. His success as a physical mathematician was phenomenal. Following Werner Heisenberg's publication of the idea of a new quantum mechanics in 1925, Dirac independently went to work on creating an appropriate new mathematics for handling it. The result was his p-q number theory, completed in 1928, a "highly original and extremely elegant mathematical technique" in which "he showed how the theories of quantum mechanics and relativity could be combined." In 1930 he published his textbook of quantum mechanics, which immediately became a classic. In 1932, at the incredibly early age of 30, he was appointed Lucrasian professor of Mathematics at Cambridge University, the chair Sir Isaac Newton had once occupied—a fitting post for one whom Niels Bohr called "the most remarkable scientific mind since Newton."

Dirac was not successful in electrical engineering, but when he entered his own domain—mathematics—he thrived and showed amazingly innovative genius. Like Dirac, everyone has a domain of his own in which he can excel. Failure in one field is no reason to lose hope: there is always another field awaiting one, in which the flower of one's destiny can flourish and thrive.

Learning from Mistakes

Alan Bond is an Australian multi-millionaire. He is the owner of the yachts that have made 4 challenges for the greatest prize in sailing, America's Cup. In 1874 he made his first challenge and was wiped out 4 nil in the best of seven series. Then, in 1977, the same thing happened. In 1980 he won one race only and was beaten

4-1. These defeats deeply disappointed him. Recalling them, he says:

'Every time I'd come home depressed, and then think, "Next time I'll know how to do it better." (*Sunday Times*, London, September 25, 1973)

Alan Bond did not waste time blaming others for his defeats. He kept on thinking what mistake it was that had led to his losing time and time again. Every defeat taught him not to repeat his mistake. He did this again and again, until eventually, in 1983, he made a challenge for the coveted trophy with a new yacht, Australia II. After being 3-1 down in the series, Australia II fought back to win by four races to three and take the cup from America for the first time in 120 years.

The best way of turning defeat into victory, in every walk of life, is to learn from one's mistakes.

Nightly Preparation for a Mighty Task

The chapter of the Qur'an entitled *"Al-Muzammil"* (The Mantled One) commences with these verses:

> "You who are wrapped up in your mantle, keep vigil all night, save for a few hours: half the night, or a little less or a little more: and with measured tone recite the Qur'an. We are about to address to you words of surpassing gravity. It is in the watches of the night that

impressions are strongest and words most certain; in the day-time you are hard-pressed with work. Remember the name of your Lord and dedicate yourself to Him utterly."

(71:1-8)

From these verses it is clear that God requires His servants to be so devoted to divine service that they rise at night in order to perform their duties to the Lord. To forgo one's sleep and spend the night hours in pursuit of a cause indicates the highest level of dedication; it shows that one has associated oneself utterly with the object of one's dedication, and will soon be in a position to represent it in the world.

This applies to worldly pursuits also. Almost all the individuals who have reached great heights in any field have been those who were willing to stay awake at night in order to gain proficiency in it.

The case of Severiano Ballesteros, the Spanish golfer, provides apt illustration of this point. Ballesteros is now indisputably one of the greatest golfers in the world and has won millions of dollars in numerous victories in tournaments on both sides of the Atlantic. There was a time, however, when he was just a poor caddy at Pedereda in Spain. He once told Frank Keating of the *Guardian* newspaper how he used to get up at night to hit a 100 or so balls "at the moon." He could not see them—"but I can tell how good and straight I hit them by the feel in hands and the sand."

To become a true Muslim is to become a personification of Islam in the eyes of the world; it is to become so associated with Islam that one is fit to carry its message to far corners of the globe. This requires intense preparation, which must be conducted in a spirit keen enough to fuel one for work through the night hours. Success does not come in mundane fields without such dedication. How, then, can it come in the field of divine service, for there is no task more difficult, and more beset by obstacles—both within and without—than that of carrying the flame of true faith in God before the world.

Accepting Defeat

In 1831, an American citizen went into business. In 1832 his business failed, so he entered the field of politics, but was no more successful in that sphere. He reverted to business in 1834, and was again a failure.

In 1841, he had a nervous breakdown. Once recovered, he again entered the political arena, in the hope that his party would nominate him as a candidate for Congress. His hopes were dashed, however, when his name failed to appear in the list of candidates. The first chance he had to run for the Senate was in 1855, but he was defeated in the election. In 1858, he once again stood in the congressional elections, and once again lost.

The name of this repeatedly unsuccessful person was Abraham Lincoln (1809-1865). So great were his services to his country that he is now known as the architect of modern America.

How did Abraham Lincoln manage to gain such a great reputation in American political and national history? How did he win his way to such a high position? According to Dr Norman Vincent Peel, the secret behind his success was that "he knew how to accept defeat."

The great secret of life is realism, and there is no form of realism greater than accepting defeat. To do so is to acknowledge the fact that, far from being ahead of others, one is behind them. In other words, it is to know where one stands in life. Once defeat is accepted, one is immediately in a position to start life's journey afresh, for such a journey can only commence from where one actually is; it cannot start from a point that one has not yet reached.

Total Involvement

Elias Howe (1819-1867) was born in Massachusetts, U.S.A. He died at the young age of 48. Although his life was short, his contribution to the world of clothes—that of the sewing machine—will always be remembered.

The sewing machine invented by Elias Howe was at first utilized, not for sewing clothes, but for stitching shoes. The main breakthrough was the development of a lock-stitch by a shuttle carrying a lower thread and a needle carrying an upper thread which passed through a hole situated at the tip of the needle.

For thousands of years, people had been accustomed to making a hole at the base of the needle. So, following the their lead, Elias Howe made the needle of his machine with a hole at the base, instead of at the tip as is now the practice. The placement of an eyelet, simple as it may seem to us now, remained a big hurdle for its inventor for quite some time. It was only a dream which finally brought about the desired solution.

As he was racking his brain to perfect his machine, Howe dreamt that he had been captured by a primitive tribe and was ordered to produce an operational sewing machine within twenty-four hours, failing which he would be speared to death. He tried hard, but could not accomplish it. When the deadline was up, the tribesmen surrounded him and raised their spears to kill him. Scared, yet still concentrating, he observed that each spear had an eyelet at the tip. He kept on gazing at the eyelet and then woke up with a start: the solution was right before him. For the machine to work, the placement of the hole had to be neither in the middle nor at the base, but at the tip. His lucky dream helped him, in 1845, to produce a sewing machine that would complete 250 stitches a minute.

What is a dream? It is the result of complete involvement. What we think about during the day, we dream about at night. Howe succeeded in inventing a machine only because he had engrossed himself in it to such an extent that he came to dream about it. Such is the case with any undertaking, whether one wants to invent a machine, or bring about a revolution in human life. One achieves success in one's aim only after complete involvement; only when the thing one has set one's mind on becomes a part of the subconscious existence that is reflected in one's dreams.

Progress in the Long Haul

In 1782, an Englishman arrived in Glasgow with a wooden printing press. With such paltry resources he began to publish a newspaper entitled the *Glasgow Advertiser*. The newspaper was later renamed the *Glasgow Herald*. Two centuries later its daily circulation had risen to 200,000 copies.

What saved John Mennons, the founder of this newspaper, from succumbing to unfavourable and adverse circumstances was his limitless enthusiasm. It more than compensated for his lack of resources. The newspaper is still going strong after a period of two centuries, in spite of serious differences between partners which arose from time to time. It was fortunate that these could always be settled amicably without the work being disrupted.

The newspaper, which was started on a wooden press, is now being printed entirely on automatic machines. The letters are neither composed nor do they undergo the process of metal infusion: the are projected on the plates by laser beam. The paper is printed and folded automatically. Then it is wrapped in polythene and taken to the despatch department. The whole process is computerised.

It was only because of its continued publication that it could benefit from all the new improved techniques which were developed at different stages. If it had ceased publication after a period of time, all the techniques would have existed, but it would have failed to utilize them.

It shows how the accomplishment of any great work requires two things in particular: limitless enthusiasm and perseverance. Obviously great works can be brought to fruition only with the help of boundless energy, enthusiasm and perseverance. Without the long, and arduous labour which is essential in any such enterprise, the survival of this paper would have been impossible.

The Greatest Asset

Lord William Wintock, British governor-general in India from 1828 to 1835, has the dubious distinction of being remembered as the man who ordered the destruction of the Taj Mahal in Agra—an order which, happily, he was never able to have carried out. This was revealed at the turn of the century by the then viceroy, Lord Curzon. The East India Company had been going through hard times, Lord Curzon explained, and it was suggested to Lord Wintock that a sale of the Taj would fetch Rs. 100,000—enough to extricate the company from its financial crisis, News of the Company's intentions circulated, and there was stiff opposition to such a move. This infuriated Lord Wintock, who now went one step further and gave orders for the total destruction of the Taj. Opposition to the imperial command stepped up, with both Hindus and Muslims joining in one massive voice of protest. The danger that full-scale rebellion would ensue if the Taj was destroyed prompted the governor-general's advisers to persuade Lord Wintock to withdraw the order.

Contemporary comment had it that "the people did not save the Taj Mahal, it was saved by its own beauty. If the Taj Mahal had not been beautiful, it would not have won such overwhelming support; Hindus and Muslims would not have united behind it to foil the British government's designs."

Had the constructors of the Taj Mahal been able to reproduce in themselves the beauty which they produced so perfectly in their work of construction, they too would have been protected by their own quality. Just as virtue in a thing wins support for its cause, so virtue in humans has the same effect. It wins one friends from the enemy camp, appreciation even from strangers. A virtuous nature is the greatest asset a person can have, for with it comes support from all quarters.

The Taj Mahal's virtue lies in its beauty, while man's beauty lies in a virtuous nature. But man's beauty should not be like that of a snake—a beautiful appearance marred by a venomous sting. How do men "sting"? By presenting a challenge to people's political and economic interests; by repeatedly resorting to violence in their dealings with others; by constantly alienating people with senseless, impulsive actions. Any virtue that one might have is cancelled out by such a "sting", and prevents one from winning people's affection.

It is the Taj Mahal's silent beauty that has won people's hearts. Who would have time for it if, in all its beauty, it tormented those who looked upon it?

All the Blood of One's Body

Professor Paul Dirac died in Florida, U.S.A., in October 1984 at the age of 84. Recipient of the Nobel Prize and many other awards, he was considered—after Newton and Einstein—the greatest scientist of modern theory—in effect the physics of the smallest part of the atom—and his effective prediction of anti-matter before it had been experimentally discovered. His "anti-matter" and "anti-universe" became the leading physical ideas for explaining the character and contents of the contemporary universe, its origin and history. J.G. Crowther's obituary to Dirac in *The Guardian* (November 4, 1984) was fittingly given the headline "Prophet of the Anti-universe."

Dirac's discovery of the first anti-particle, known as a positron, revolutionized the world of nuclear physics. Students were naturally interested to know how he arrived at this world-shaking discovery. His answers often proved somewhat disconcerting. "When people asked him how he got his startling ideas about the nature of sub-atomic matter," Crowther writes, "he would patiently explain that he did so by lying on his study floor with his feet up so that the blood ran to his head."

Dirac's answer might appear tongue-in-cheek, but in fact what he said was quite true. Great intellectual feats can only be accomplished by letting all the blood of one's body run to one's head—by channelling all one's energy into the intellectual pursuit one had undertaken.

Few people actually do this. They rather tend to diversify their efforts. Their failure to concentrate on a single goal renders all their efforts incomplete and ineffective. Every worthwhile task demands all the strength that an individual can muster. The only way to be successful in one's work is to give it all one has.

After Being Broken

The atom is the final unit of matter, just as the individual is the final unit of society. If one succeeds in breaking an atom one does not destroy it; rather one converts it into a greater force, known as atomic energy. Matter is energy in a solid form and energy matter in a dispersed form. When the atoms of matter are broken and converted into atomic energy, they are transformed into a force much more potent than in their material form.

A locomotive consumes two tons of coal in seventy miles; a motorcar uses up a gallon of petrol every twenty to forty miles. But when uranium weighting just twelve pounds is converted into atomic energy, it is able to convey a high-speed rocket on a 40,000 mile journey into space. That's how great the difference is between ordinary material energy and atomic energy.

So it is with that unit of society known as man. When man is 'broken,' his horizons expand vastly. Just as breakage does not destroy matter, so defeat does not ruin man. Matter increases in strength when broken up. So man, when defeated, gains new, increased strength.

When man is beset by defeat, his inner forces are released. His senses are aroused. His concealed strength comes to the fore and he sets about redressing his setback. Spurred on with new resolve and determination, he devotes himself to the task of regaining what has been lost. An irresistible spirit arises within him. Nothing can arrest his advance. Like a river flowing to the sea, he surmounts every obstacle in relentless pursuit of his goal.

The occurrence of an atomic explosion in matter turns it into a vastly more powerful substance. The human personality, too, contains huge, latent potential. This potential bursts out into the open when there is an eruption within one's soul. It breaks free when some shattering disaster afflicts one. The strings that have held one down are torn apart and begin to vibrate to the tune of life.

Recognizing Oneself

God has a special purpose for every individual human being. To be born into this world is to make a promise to God that one will spend one's life fulfilling the purpose that God intends for one. The worth of every human being lies in his faithfulness to this promise.

God has endowed every individual with certain talents. These talents may be inborn, or they may develop at a later stage in life. It is for every human being to recognize where his talents lie, and then make use of them, thereby enacting the role that God has singled out for him. One who recognizes himself in this way has taken up his true place in God's pattern of creation, while one who fails to do so will find himself at odds—not only with himself—but with the whole of creation.

This can be illustrated by the respective cases of two companions of the Prophet Muhammad. Abu Huraira was one of the companions, and Khalid, the son of Walid, another. No less than 5,374 traditions (sayings of the Prophet) have been related on the authority of Abu Huraira, while less than one hundred can be traced back to Khalid. Extraordinary as this disparity may seem, all it indicates is a difference in the arena in which they worked. It does not mean that one of them did more for Islam than the other.

Abu Huraira and Khalid were both sincere, dedicated Muslims. But as regards talents, they were very different from each other. Each of them awoke to his separate vocation in life, and followed it implicitly. In accordance with his own particular abilities, Abu Huraira picked one arena in which to serve the cause of Islam, while Khalid picked another, equally suitable one, for himself.

Before Khalid became a Muslim, he took part in several military campaigns against Islam. He later told of how he used to fight with the feeling the he had "adopted a mistaken stance"—that he was fighting for the wrong cause. His conscience continued to haunt him, until shortly before the conquest of Mecca, when he went to Medina and accepted Islam.

Khalid was by nature exceptionally brave and courageous. He recognized this quality of his, and saw how to use it to full effect. By becoming fully aware of himself, he recognized the special part that had been delegated to him on the vast stage of the Islamic arena. He determined to use the courage God had given him to destroy polytheistic religion, and establish monotheism in its place.

Khalid, therefore, dedicated the rest of his life to active service in the cause of Islam. Continually he would ask God to make him strong and steadfast in this path, and he also used to ask God's Prophet to pray for him. So great were his services to Islam that the Prophet called Khalid "one of God's swords, drawn against the idolators."

As for Abu Huraira, he did not have the same qualities as Khalid. What he did have, however, was a prodigious memory. Recognizing where his talents lay, he resolved to use them in the service of Islam.

It is related in the Hadith that Abu Huraira once asked the Prophet to pray that God should give him knowledge which he would not forget. The Prophet said "Amen" to that, and prayed as Abu Huraira had requested. Abu Huraira's exceptional memory was both a result of the Prophet's prayer for him, and also of his own eagerness to serve Islam in the way most suited to his talents and temperament.

Under the protective wing of such prayers, he devoted himself heart and soul to the area to which he was assigned. Spending as much time as he could in the company of the Prophet, he listened attentively to what was said, memorizing it and—when the need arose—

writing it down. By recognizing where his own talents lay, and in doing all he could to develop them, he has taken his place in Islamic history as the greatest original relator of the sayings of the Prophet Muhammad.

Every person has a responsibility to first recognize himself—to see where his own talents lie and do all he can to channel them in a positive direction. By doing this one is benefiting, not only oneself, but even more the cause to which one is committed.

Social Behaviour

A certain Mr Ajwani was appointed as a sales representative in a large pharmaceuticals firm in Calcutta in 1965. His predecessor had been engaged at a monthly salary of Rs 1,200 plus rail expenses. Mr Ajwani made it clear that the would not accept less than Rs 3,000 per month and that he would only agree to travel by air when he had to visit other towns to take orders. The director who was interviewing him pointed out that, in terms of his total expenses, that was much too much. But Mr Ajwani replied, "I will give you 'much too much' work in return. Just give me a chance and you will see". There was something very engaging about the way he put his arguments, and finally he was appointed as the firm's representative for the area of Gujarat.

In those days a certain famous lady doctor had a

flourishing practice in one of the towns of Gujarat, but although her clinic required great quantities of medicines, she refused point blank to meet pharmaceuticals agents if they were males. It had so happened that an agent had once used his knowledge of palmistry as a pretext to hold her hand and then kiss it. After this very disturbing affair, she had come to feel apprehensive about the behaviour of other agents, and refused to allow any of them even to enter her clinic.

When Mr Ajwani was on the point of setting off on a business trip which was to take him to this very city, he told his director that the was confident that he would get orders from this lady doctor. The director told him not to be so naive, for everyone knew that this was a sheer impossibility. Her attitude was so well-known that none of the agents had the remotest hope of ever meeting her, far less of receiving orders from her.

Undaunted, Mr Ajwani set off. In the plane, he found himself seated next to an elderly lady who was obviously of a good family. They had hardly taken off when the old lady had a sudden fit of coughing. Some sputum came into her mouth and she became quite flustered. Mr Ajwani, seeing how awkward she felt, quickly placed his handkerchief in front of her mouth so that she could spit into it. Then he went to the bathroom and dispose of it. His thoughtfulness impressed her greatly and they chatted amicably for the rest of the flight. When the plane landed, they disembarked together, he helping her with her hand luggage. On coming out of the 'arrivals' lounge, she was distressed to discover that no car had come to receive her. Mr Ajwani once again offered to be of help, saying that he could easily drop her at her home by taxi before going on to his hotel. She gratefully agreed to this and, on reaching home, made a note of his name and address before saying goodbye to him.

Shortly afterwards, her daughter came back home and was surprised to find her mother there. She felt very sorry that the message about her arrival had never reached her, and that her mother had had no car to receive her and bring her home. "You must have had difficulty in coming home alone," she said to her mother. "Not at all," the old lady replied, and, her eyes shining with gratitude, she told her the whole story of the kind gentleman she had met on the plane. The daughter was very favourably impressed and immediately telephoned Mr Ajwani at his hotel to thank him and invite him to dinner. Mr Ajwani promptly accepted her invitation, and, when they were introduced to each other, he discovered, to his great surprise, that she was none other than the famous lady doctor who hated male agents. When she learnt that Mr Ajwani represented a pharmaceuticals company, she lost no time in placing a sizeable order with him, and added that since she always needed large quantities of medicines in her clinic, he could take it that she would be a regular customer and that he could keep sending her supplies every month.

After dinner, he immediately trunk-called his boss from his hotel to give him the good news. His boss could hardly believe his ears and thought at first that he must be joking. But two days later, he thought quite differently when he received the cheque and the order signed by her.

On a subsequent occasion when I had occasion to meet Mr Ajwani, I asked him, just by the way, to give me some good business tips. He replied, "Polite conversation and gentlemanly behaviour." I added, "Yes, even when there appears to be no obvious advantage!"

Polite behaviour falls into two categories. One follows the conventional etiquette reserved for relatives, acquaintances and people with whom one's interests are associated. It is socially beneficial in that it makes relationships easier, smoother and more generally civilized. Even if such behaviour is sometimes artificial, it has a certain positive, social value. The other kind of good behaviour is completely natural, straight from the heart and based on genuine consideration for others. When it becomes a matter of habit with people from all walks of life, it is of inestimable value in all human relations. It is not, of course, something which one "switches on" in the hopes of immediate reward, but is something rather which eventually benefits one in innumerable, often intangible, ways, simply because it makes for social harmony at its best.

Life's Labours are Never Lost

Jana Devangaddy of Bangalore was a student at Cambridge when Jawahar Lal Nehru went to study there. He developed a close association with Nehru. It was because of this relationship that his son, Deren Angaddy, heard a lot about Nehru during his childhood. Impressed with his personality, Deren used to impersonate him. Later Deren became a film actor.

When Attenborough planned to produce a film on Gandhi, with an investment of about $ 25 million. Deren was selected to play the role of Nehru. However, after six months he was told by the film producers that he was being dropped from the list of actors and that Roshan Seth had been chosen to play this role instead. This decision was made six months after Deren Angaddy had been offered the role, during which time he had worked hard to perfect his role. The news shocked him to the point where he committed suicide.

Why did Deren Angaddy take such a drastic step? Was it because he had worked hard to develop an ability which had no further use? Seemingly this had plunged him into a depression so deep that he took his life.

People tend to overlook the fact that professional skill and ability achieved by hard struggle is an investment in itself. Even if they fail to find an immediate outlet, life's labours are never lost in the long run. Sooner or later opportunities are bound to present themselves to draw on such painfully acquired skills.

An Economic Pearl Harbour

In December 1941, during the second world war, the U.S.A.'s top naval base, Pearl Harbour, on the Pacific island of Hawaii, was attacked without prior warning by the Japanese. So severe was the bombardment that, of the hundred odd naval vessels anchored there, only a handful survived. This had the immediate effect of bringing America into the war as one of the Allied Powers. Up till that point, the U.S.A. had had no direct involvement in hostilities save as a supplier of armaments to the enemies of Japan. The Japanese attack had been uncalled-for and ill-considered, but they did not realize the magnitude of their error until 1945, when America finally took its revenge by dropping the first-ever atom bombs on two of Japan's major industrial centres, Hiroshima and Nagasaki, thus annihilating Japan as a military power. The Americans then kept a tight military and political hold over Japan. But the latter country, astonishingly, recuperated from the horror of large-scale atomic devastation, and proceeded to adapt itself to an entirely new set of circumstances. Before the second world war, it had relied on the power of weapons. But after witnessing the destruction they caused, it relinquished their use and set about reconstructing the country along entirely peaceful lines. Having once adopted this course, the Japanese showed great versatility, resilience and assiduity, and their success has been such that Japan is now considered the second greatest industrial power in the entire world today. Its trade surplus is 37 billion dollars, more even than that of the U.S.A. In the field of industry, the victors have been defeated by the vanquished. Simply by accepting the fact that aggression could not pay dividends and then channelizing its potential within the field of industry, Japan has managed quite miraculously to supersede all the other nations of the world.

The Americans are greatly upset at this state of affairs and refer to the present 'invasion' of Japanese goods as an Economic Pearl Harbour. A book recently published in America, under the title of "Japan-Number One", has become a best-seller. It clearly shows that Japan has far outrun the U.S.A. in business and will soon supersede Britain. So far as foreign exchange is concerned, Japan is the wealthiest country in the world, its foreign exchange reserves totalling 74 billion dollars in 1984. (*The Times of India*, 13-14 June, 1985).

How did Japan turn its military defeat into an economic victory? By encouraging patience and perservance and avoiding provocation, it concentrated its energies on peaceful (and, of course, remunerative) fields, rather than indulge in retaliatory violence. It initially accepted the military and political supremacy of other nations, quickly adapting itself to new scales of values, then set about the economic rehabilitation of the country without wasting a single moment on bewailing lost opportunities, blaming others for its misfortunes or on pointless nostalgia. Rather than make further mistakes—Pearl Harbour having been the worst—it concentrated all of its attention on seizing existing opportunities. In short, Japan accepted the blame for its own destruction, and, once having done so, was able seriously to launch itself on its own economic uplift.

We must never lose sight of the fact that we are not lone travellers on this earth. There are always others who are trying to race ahead of us in this world of competition. The resulting situation can be approached in two entirely different ways. One is to collide with anything which obstructs our path. The other is to circumvent obstacles and then to go on our way. Clearly, the first is self-destructive, while the second, in avoiding confrontations, is much more likely to prove advantageous. A ship which sails straight at a rock or an iceberg is doomed to disaster. It is the ship which veers temporarily off its course to avoid the reefs which will eventually sail safely into harbour. Similarly, Japan, by giving up ideas of military supremacy, has reached a much more worthwhile objective—economic supremacy.

It is worth remembering that Hiroshima and Nagasaki, once symbols of Japan's total annihilation as a military power, are now symbols, forty years later, of Japan's stunning economic success.

Having One's Share

The Bata Shoe Company is named after the family which founded it. Originally the Bata family lived in Czechoslovakia, where they began manufacturing shoes as far back as 1620. Thomas Bata Senior, father of the present proprietor, established a shoe factory for the first time in 1925. His career was cut short though when his private plane lost its bearings in heavy fog and crashed, burning him to death on the spot. On his father's death, Thomas Bata Junior became president of Bata Ltd.

The Bata Company, the largest shoe manufacturer in the world, is now doing business in 114 different countries, having sold 315 million pairs of shoes throughout the world in 1982. Its greatest volume of business is in Canada, with India ranking second. It has 90 thousand direct employees, not to mention thousands of indirect employees.

Mr. Thomas Bata Junior visited India for the fortieth time in 1983. On this occasion, a correspondent asked him what he thought was the most important factor in his success. Mr Bata replied, "In manufacturing shoes which range from cheap to costly, we take special care to fulfill the actual needs of our consumers. We do, in fact, look after our customers better than anyone else."

What we learn from the Bata Shoe Company's success is that if you want to take, you should try to give. It is only in giving to others that we can have our share too.

Message Without Words

A certain student from Rajasthan had failed in his high school examinations. He appeared again the following year, but failed again. After having failed for the third time the next year he was so ashamed of his performance that he left his home, unable to show his face to his family.

He just kept walking about aimlessly. After a long time he stopped at a well to quench his thirst. Women and children had gathered around it, filling their pots by turns. There he caught sight of something. Something small, but of great significance. He was deeply moved, and his thirst was gone. All of a sudden he felt as though he had found something far greater than the water he had come for. What happened was quite simple. The villagers who visited the well for water, usually brought two earthen pots. They would place one pot on a stone near the well while letting the other down on a rope inside the well to draw water. To his astonishment, the part of the stone on which the pot was placed had rubbed away and there was a hollow there. The pot was made of earth, he thought, but when it was placed on the same spot over and over again, it had worn away the stone which was a far harder a substance. The strong element had given way to the weak, just through constant action. "Then why should I not succeed in my examinations if I too persevere? I can surely overcome my shortcomings by putting greater effort into my studies!"

Such thoughts brought him to a halt. He immediately decided to go back home and start working hard on his studies once again. The following year he appeared for the fourth time in his high school examinations. This time the result, astonishingly, was the opposite of the previous one. He had done his papers so well this time that he had first class marks. After having failed three times he had finally distinguished himself. The lesson of the stone had worked like a miracle and this had altered his attitude altogether. The same student who had run away from home, unable to face defeat, had come to stand first in all the examinations he took. When he topped in his M.A. examinations, he was given a scholarship to study abroad and from there he took his doctorate.

This may be a solitary instance that occurred in an isolated village, but, indeed, in every place there exists such a "stone" which, by pointing out man's shortcomings and failures, can teach him a lesson provided he shows sufficient receptiveness to the message it conveys. It he only cares to look, he will find around him some such "stone" which will set him on the right course again.

Working One's Way Up

A man entered a certain recruiting office and said, "I want to join as a soldier."

"But how old are you?" the sergeant asked.

"Sixty," was the man's reply

"You know quite well that sixty is too old for you to become a soldier."

"All right, if 60 is too old for a soldier, don't you need any generals?"

If one wants to start one's career as a general, one will be hard put to it to do so. It's just like a race where one can't leap straight from the starting point to the finishing line. To succeed in anything, we have to be like the tree, starting from the seed, growing slowly and putting out branches, twigs, leaves and flowers when the appropriate times come around. Similarly, business starts with investing money, not with earning profits. The construction of a house starts with the laying of the foundation, not with the tiling of the roof. The factory begins with the acquisition of machinery and not with the sale of the end products. Congregational matters are very much on a parallel. They begin from the inculcation in individuals of a sense of purpose and an understanding of the importance of hard work, honesty, endurance and unity.

Not until the individuals of a nation are imbued with these important ideals to a very high degree can measures be taken for the advancement of the cause. If we ignore the importance of preconditioning, our missionary ventures are bound to end in failure. Any attempt to launch a movement without a solid, national infrastructure would be like trying to roof a house without raising its walls. A roof put up in this way is bound eventually to collapse on one's head. In much the same way, any steps taken before individuals have been properly prepared for them will lead inevitably to failure and chaos—even death and destruction. They will be found to lead only further and further away from the true objectives.

Warding off Danger

I once went to spend a few days at a religious institution situated on the outskirts of Alwar, a city in Rajasthan. To the one side there extended the buildings of the city and , to the other, there were open fields stretching far and wide. During my stay there, I went out one evening at sunset to have a walk in the fields.

Unfortunately, after I had gone some distance, I was rushed at by a pack of dogs all barking and snarling. I had to throw stones at them to chase them away. On my return, I mentioned to my host how I had almost been set upon by these animals. My host, Maulana Mufti Jamaluddin Qasmi, who presides over the institution, simply smiled and said, "All right, I'll come with you tomorrow." The following day, we set off together, the Maulana having armed himself with a stick which was quite long enough to be visible from afar. When we reached the spot where I had come upon the dogs the day before, they were there all right, but, there was not so much as a whimper out of them, far less a bark. Not one of them made a move to rush at us. So we passed by undisturbed. On our way back, they were still there, but, they did not create a commotion this time either, and we reached home without any untoward incidents, "That was the miracle of the big stick," said the Maulana with a smile. "Yesterday you were unarmed, so those wretched curs dared to attack. Today it was a very different story, for the dogs, immediately realizing that you were well-equipped to deal with them, lost courage and gave up any idea they had of attacking. A dog will attack you only if he thinks you are vulnerable. But he would not do so if he found you armed."

There are certain of the human species too, who sadly, will behave well only when you have a 'big stick' in your hand. But the moment they find you defenseless, they become bold. They are the type of people who are brave when dealing with those weaker than themselves, and who are out and out cowards when confronted with anyone stronger. This unfortunate state of affairs calls for people to be well-equipped to deal effectively with such unworthy individuals. In society, one ought, in principle, to be peaceable, humble and courteous to all. But, to be practical, one should be well armed to meet adverse situations, so that others are discouraged at the outset from harming one. Where would all our beautiful roses be, if nature had not provided them with innumerable thorns?

Aiming High

Several disgruntled Muslim youths stood in an agitated group outside the University Offices, loudly bewailing the fact that they had not been admitted to the various academic courses they had chosen. Without exception, they blamed circumstances for their failure to gain entry to the University. Some also blamed the environment for their having remained out of work for so long. An elderly gentleman, who was sitting close by, could not help overhearing their lamentations. Finally, he could contain himself no longer, and he jumped up and said to them, "I am sure you feel your complaints are well-founded, but, why compete at a level where the seats are all bound to be taken already? That will get you nowhere. You should attempt to enter at the top, for that is where you will find the vacant seats. Produce distinctive qualifications and there will be no question of your being rejected. There are always places at the top for people of merit. Be you student, businessman, lawyer or doctor, try to distinguish yourself in whatever field you have chosen, for that is the sure way to success. Even if it is only something like a mousetrap that you have the reputation for making well, people will come knocking at your door for it. The real mistake is to produce the same quality of goods with which the market is already flooded. It is pointless to do this, then complain about being discriminated against. If you work hard and bend your brains to producing something superior in design and quality to what is already on the market, people will flock to buy it.

"No society is ever free of prejudice and narrow-mindedness; it is just one unfortunate aspect of community-living. The difference in this from one society to another is only one of degree. But these are barriers which can definitely be surmounted through diligence and application. Let us suppose that you have passed an examination with 45 percent marks, giving you a very slight advantage over a rival who only has forty percent. In such a case, it is quite conceivable that prejudice could come in your way, and your application could be rejected in favour of your rival's. But let us suppose that you had eighty percent marks. All the walls of prejudice would then have to crumble and fall in the face of superior talent. No one would then dare deny you your rights. Does it not make sense then to try your hardest to reach the highest pinnacles of academic success? It is only a question of working much harder than your rival. Then the world will be convinced that you have not only set yourself the highest standards, but have also lived up to them.

Once launched upon life with superior knowledge and skills, there is no question of your failing to find the place you deserve. Every door will open to you, because it is invariably the highly qualified who are in demand."

The Flight of the Bee

The bees make their hives at one place, but often have to travel many miles to other places to suck the nectar from the flowers. Sometimes they have to keep flying the whole day in order to do so, and observation of the bees has shown that when they leave home in the early morning, it is still dark, but that when they set off home in the evening, the sun has not yet set and it is still light. To leave in the morning darkness and return in the evening light is a very practical thing to do, because travelling in the morning means moving from dark to light while travelling in the evening means moving from light to dark. The bee takes into account the time-span between its arrival and departure and makes its journeys accordingly. It knows that it can travel to distant parts without losing its way provided it does so in the daylight, but it can start its journey in darkness because it knows that daylight is not far away. Similarly, it avoids the possibility of going astray in the dark by being as close as possible to its hive in the evening when darkness is about to fall, so it sets off on its last journey home while it is still light.

Nature teaches us a lesson through the bees. It shows us that each of our steps should be based on realities and not on wishful thinking or vague suppositions. The future will, of necessity, have its moments of darkness as well as its moments of light. If we fail to note the significance of this difference and begin our journeys in ignorance and without forethought, the future will hold little that is bright for us. Moments of light and dark will come according to their own set course, and not as a result of our wishful thinking. If we do not pay need to the realities of existence and plan our lives accordingly, we shall have the illusion that we are heading towards a bright future and splendid results, whereas, when the next moment of darkness arrives, we shall discover that, all along, we had been heading towards darkness.

Teaching the Teachers

For about twenty years, between 1950 and 1970, Japan used to import superior industrial technology from the west, at times by outright purchase, but more often by borrowing, or on a credit basis. As a result,

Japan today stands on its own feet economically and is in a position to export not only its goods but also its know-how to other countries. Thanks to its advanced technical expertise, it now has the opportunities to help other countries, enter into friendly relations with them and draw up contracts to do business with them. Some of their feats include working on the latest irrigation projects in Thailand, giving instruction in computer programming in Singapore, constructing iron and steel factories in South Korea and China, and setting up petro-chemical industries in the Middle East, etc. The Japanese learnt iron and steel making from the Americans and have now developed it so extensively that they are at present exporting their skills to the Americans themselves. Japan, once the learner, is now so well placed in so many fields—particularly in communication and electronics, that America is seeking its technical assistance in many of its important military departments. The students are now teaching their teachers. A newspaper correspondent reports: "Now the flow is out instead of in." (*The Hindustan Times*, June 11, 1981)

Japan willingly submitted to industrial tutelage for 20 years and, as a result, has attained the position of industrial dominance that it occupies today. If it had chosen not to recognise the supremacy of others at that crucial point in its development, and had felt too proud to go to them for help, it could never have had such resounding successes.

All too often, we have to lose in order to gain. We have to resign ourselves to our lowly position until we can work ourselves up to more satisfactory heights. Those who recognise this necessity as one of the facts of life will have a better chance of succeeding in this world than those who expect to be able to climb straight to the top without first having accepted a position of humility, or who persist in blaming others for their failures. Patience, fortitude and tenacity are the virtues which will see us through to success, provided they are always leavened by humility.

Keeping Calm in the Face of Adversity

When Napoleon Buonaparte (1769-1821) escaped from the Island of Elba after his first term of imprisonment, he was accompanied only by a small group of loyal soldiers. Once dethroned, he now again aspired to the throne of France. But in the very first encounter, he found himself face to face with 20,000 French soldiers.

Napoleon, although considered one of the most courageous leaders the world has known, avoided a direct confrontation with his opponents. He did not make the mistake of foolishly ignoring his own military weakness. At the crucial moment, when he and his little band of men stood face to face with this enormous army, he stepped forward, completely unarmed and stood calmly before his enemies. Then with great composure he unbuttoned his coat and bared his chest. In a voice now charged with emotion he addressed the great throng of soldiers—many of whom had served under him in the past: "Which one of you is willing to fire at the naked chest of his father?" The battlefield rang with shouts of 'No one!' Almost all of the soldiers belonging to the enemy camp rushed to the side of Napolean, who emerged victorious and once more ascended the throne of France. If, in the destitute state he was in at that time, he had attempted to do battle with the French army, he would surely have been slaughtered on that very battlefield.

Whatever a man's resources, if he has to deal effectively with a situation, he must be able to make a proper assessment of it. And this he will not be able to do if he panics in the face of danger. It is only if he does not lose his nerve and keeps his mind open to what is practical that he will be able to overcome the obstacles in his path. Inevitably, his success depends upon his being able to make a well-considered choice of whatever material and mental resources are available to him and then putting them to proper use. History abounds in instances of the weak overcoming the strong, simply by strategic deployments of resources. The reason for such success is not far to seek: often the enemy is not a as strong as he appears to be. Everyone has his Achilles heel. It is just a question of finding it and then ruthlessly exploiting it. Just as Napolean exploited the French troops' old and sentimental loyalty to himself—that being his only mainstay—so can ordinary individuals take advantage of their enemies' vulnerability in order to gain their point without the kind of confrontation which could be disastrous to both sides.

Seeking the Right Alternatives

A luckless passenger rushed, panting, into the station just as his train was steaming out. His watch—unaccountably slow by ten minutes—had let him down. "Don't worry, Babuji," sympathised a passing porter, there will be another train along in about a couple of hours. Why go away? Just wait here for it on this same platform." The passenger, keen to reach his destination, decided to accept his advice, even if it meant waiting two, long tedious hours. Just getting to where he wanted to go was too important to him to think of expending time and energy coming and going from the station all over again, and perhaps missing his train once again, so he stayed right where he was and catch his train he did.

When we miss a train, there is always the comforting knowledge that there is that next train coming along. That is the lesson that the platform teaches. It is then up to us to make the correct decision about our next move. But it is surprising how many people fail to grasp this reality. They are inexplicably plunged into gloom and depression when they fail initially to grasp an opportunity, and frequently adopt such a pessimistic attitude that they fritter away their precious energies in blaming others for their failures. How much better it would be if they were to make a proper assessment of the situation, taking all possibilities into account, and then seek new ways and means of achieving their goals, even if it means a lengthy wait. This is a matter simply of patience and determination. There is always that "next train" for them to catch. It is just a question of being properly alert to this, and being ready to avail of that God-given second opportunity.

If, in any given situation, someone with whom you have business or personal relations turns hostile, pursuing a policy of open confrontation seldom reaps rewards. It is almost invariably more politic to extend courtesy, love and sympathy. That is the way to a person's heart. It is only by pursuing such a course that a formidable foe may be transformed into a faithful friend.

Suppose you work in an office and, for reasons which you fail to comprehend, you are dismissed. In such a situation, if initial attempts to clear your name and have yourself honourably reinstated come to naught, it is seldom worthwhile persisting in your efforts. It is far better to wash your hands of the whole situation and try to break new ground elsewhere. That way you can sometimes do even better than before.

Often when someone does not pay you your dues, your first inclination is to enter into legal battles with him, or wage a relentless psychological war on him. Either course should be eschewed, for the net result is generally wasted time and money. Years can go by without your receiving anything in return for a great deal of energy spent. No, it is better to ignore the injustice done to you, and to put your trust in hard work to get what you want out of life. It is perfectly possible that, through sheer diligence, you will succeed in achieving all those things you wanted others to give you as a matter of right.

Most personal problems are the result of a limited outlook on life. If people were to broaden their perspectives, they would soon realize that there are many different ways of approaching the same problem. It would, above all, become clear to them that things which are impossible to obtain by direct confrontation can be achieved by the patient fostering of mutual goodwill. Where provocation and retaliation have failed, patience and human concern will succeed.

In Giving We Receive

*M*r. Surjit Singh Lamba (b. 1931) who works in the Law Ministry and lives in Kirti Nagar, New Delhi, has been gifted by nature with a photographic memory. This means that just by reading anything a few times, be it prose or poetry, he can remember all of its details.

He demonstrated this skill when he visited our office in June, 1983, by reproducing whole articles of Al-Risala from memory.

Being a great admirer of Iqbal, he has learnt hundreds and thousands of his verses by heart, thus becoming a specialist on his life and works. In 1983, Mr Lamba went to Pakistan where he was hailed as an authority on Iqbal. One Mr Amir Hussain of Lahore, who is also renowned as an expert on Iqbal, challenged Mr Lamba to recite more verses by heart than he could himself. So convinced was Amir Hussain Lahori of his superiority, that he offered to hand over Rs 5000 in cash to Mr Lamba if he could beat him. Mr Lamba accepted the challenge, and it was agreed that, turn about, each would recite any verse from any part of any poem by Iqbal and that the other should have to recite whatever followed. Mr Lamba was able to recite faultlessly whatever followed on from Amir Hussain's cues. But Amir Husain was ultimately unable to match his performance, and so lost the contest. Explaining his prowess, Mr Lamba remarked, "I have been hovering around the candle of Iqbal like a moth for the past ten years. It is only if you have hovered around it more than I have that you will be able to outdo me in recitation."

It is only such utter devotion—no matter what the field of activity—which can lead to success. There are few things in life which cannot be likened to the candle. Only those who have hovered around it more than others in this world of struggle and competition can aspire to advance in life. It is by putting everything we have—brains, effort, talent, money, energy—into whatever we are doing, that we can hope to derive some benefit from it. And never can we hope to receive more than we have actually given.

Beware of Negative Thinking

The greatest weakness of present-day Muslims is their negative psychology. They feel that all the nations of the world are inimical to them, and so many of their activities are seen as acts of hostility against the Muslims. This negative psychology has resulted in all their thinking becoming unrealistic. Suppose you are hit on the head by a ripe piece of fruit which has fallen down from a tree. If you persist in thinking that the tree has maliciously thrown it down at you, you will never succeed in either identifying the problem or in solving it.

The U.S.A., for instance, takes the side of the Israeli Jews against the Palestinian Muslims. All over the world, Muslims see this as an expression of enmity towards themselves. But nothing could be further from the truth. In this world of vested interests, America sides with Israel, because its own economic interests are at stake there. It has nothing to do with being an enemy of the Muslims.

By helping Israel, America makes a two-fold gain. Firstly, it can in this way keep the oil-producing countries under continuous pressure, so that they are left with no choice but to come to terms with American conditions at the negotiating table. Secondly, benefits definitely accrue to America in the realm of finance. The most lucrative business of the developed countries is the granting of "aid" to the weaker and the developing countries, and the receiving of interest on the amounts loaned. The actual amount to be repaid is in easy installments, but the payment of interest has to be made in full each year. Such loans are granted for various kinds of development work, but the major share of it goes towards buying modern military equipment, which is a highly profitable affair for the U.S.A., it being the chief supplier. The perpetual state of war between the Arabs and Israel is excellent for American business because, they can then sell costly weapons to Israel against loans, and receive in return huge amounts of interest. According to a recent report, the amount of loan interest that Israel repays to America is of the order of 910 million dollars a year. And the money paid out for the costly weapons that the Arabs buy from America is over and above what Israel pays the U.S.A.

Before indulging in negative thinking, Muslims should consider that, in diplomacy, there are no real friends or enemies. There are only economic interests.

Ducking Below the Waves

Two young friends, both good swimmers, once went swimming off the coast of Madras. The day was pleasant, the sea calm, and sometimes skimming along the surface, sometimes plunging below, they had soon left the shore far behind. Then, quite without warning, they found themselves struggling against enormous waves which bore down on them with tremendous force. One of the young men struck out strongly against the waves, battling his way to the shore. But try as he might, he could not make the distance to the beach and he was drowned. The waves had proved stronger than he. His friend also struck out in the same way, but soon realized his efforts would be futile. Luckily, he remembered that the force of the waves was felt more on the surface and much less underneath, so he immediately plunged, kicking and struggling, to a depth where he was no longer buffeted about. Now he began literally to swim for his life, his lungs bursting and his muscles aching. By straining every fibre of his being, he managed to reach the shallows, where he was picked up unconscious by some sailors. They brought him safely to dry land, where he was taken to hospital. He was given emergency treatment and soon recovered. It had certainly been lucky for him that there had been a boat in the vicinity to haul him out, and that he could have immediate medical attention. But what had really saved his life was his change of tactics when he realized that the waves were going to be too powerful for him.

Both the young men had struggled valiantly to survive, but it was the one who had not depended only on physical strength but also on his intelligence who lived to tell the tale. He had understood almost immediately that a confrontation of his own human strength with the enormous powers of nature would be inane and futile.

This is a principle which might well be applied to the whole spectrum of human activity, for confrontation seldom brings us anything positive. When a typhoon approaches, even the fishes dive deep.

Constructive Temperament

Dr. Abdul Jalil of New Delhi, once had the opportunity to visit Japan in 1970, where he stayed for six months. He later recounted an incident to me which cast a significant light on the Japanese character. It seems that during his stay in Tokyo, he would often take a 15 minute ride on a suburban train to a place just outside the city. One day, when the fifteen minutes had passed and there was no sign of his station, he began to feel uneasy. Sure enough, when the train stopped, it was at some other station, and he realized that somehow or the other he had boarded the wrong train at Tokyo. In some agitation he tried to get help from the Japanese who was sitting next to him, but since neither could speak the others language, conversation was impossible. Dr Jalil then thought of writing down the name of his station in block capitals and showing it to his travelling companion. The Japanese could apparently read that much and promptly pulled the communication cord to stop the train, which had just begun to move out of the station. He hurried Dr. Jalil off the train and took him to another platform which was for trains going in the opposite direction. There he put Dr. Jalil on the right train, and, in spite of the fact that no conversation was possible, insisted on accompanying him to his destination. Only then did he take his leave and go off to board another train which would take him on his way.

Another incident he recounted was that of a car accident which he witnessed himself as he walked along the pavements of Tokyo. Two cars, both driven by Japanese, had collided The two drivers immediately got out of their cars and stood facing each other with heads bowed. Both said: "It's my fault. Please, forgive me."

Only people with a constructive temperament could behave in such a self-abnegating way. A temperament such as this is a major guarantee of a nation's success. By contrast, individuals who care for nothing but their own selfish interests can neither achieve personal success, nor can they make any contribution to the building of their nation.

Perseverance Pays

Wakening up in the morning to the noisy chirruping of the birds, the man noticed a broken egg lying on the ground. It had obviously fallen from a nest built by sparrows just under the ceiling of his modest dwelling. Wearily he removed the broken egg, then, noting with disgust the straws which were eternally littering his floor, he stood up on a piece of furniture, and swiped the nest out of its niche. Then he spent quite some time and effort cleaning up the whole place.

The very next day, he found more straws dirtying his newly cleaned floor and, looking up, he saw that the birds were again building their nest under his roof. He felt he was going mad with their chirruping and the perpetual mess they made, so he destroyed the new nest before it was even half-completed. That way he thought he could drive them away forever.

But the tragedy of the devastated nest only spurred the birds on to greater efforts, and showing great daring, they worked faster then ever. They did not waste a single moment on lamenting their loss. Nor did they go away to collect a whole flock of birds to come and make a united attack on the house owner. They simply flew to and from the home, quietly and incessantly picking up fresh straws and fixing them in position. They did not waste a single moment.

This self-same story was repeated from day to day

for over a month. The house owner would angrily destroy their home and moments later the sparrows would reappear with straws in their beaks to begin their labour all over again. Their efforts seemed fruitless. Their incessant gathering of straws was apparently futile. But regardless of consequences, they went on steadily with their work. It was the birds' answer to the unmitigated hatred of the man. Yet although he was the stronger, they always seemed somehow to foil him. And, finally their silent endeavours gained the upper hand. The man realized that his resistance was futile and he stopped destroying the nests. Now they have completed their nest and have successfully laid and hatched their eggs. Their chirruping no longer incenses the man. He has simply ceased to mind them, for they have taught him a priceless lesson —never hate your enemy. In all circumstances, persevere steadfastly in constructive activities. In the end you will emerge victorious.

Ease Always Comes After Hardship

Anyone who has experienced a dust or sand storm in desert regions will know how traumatic this can be. There does not appear to be anything good about the scorching, blinding winds. But Soviet meteorologists have made investigations, in the Karakoram desert into the properties of dust storms and found that they are nature's way of controlling extreme climates. The strong winds raise the dust up to form a screen in the atmosphere, guarding the earth from the intensity of the sun's heat. The surface of the desert, scalded by the summer sun, is considerably cooled when it erupts in a dust storm. Sometimes the resultant change of temperature can be felt, say, in America and the Arctic, far afield as these areas are from Arabia, and Central Asia.

Such is the order of nature. In this world just as ease always follows hardship, so fruitful results come only from arduous, painstaking processes. This is the way nature works, and from it we can see how we should live on earth. We should be prepared for a period of hard struggle before we can expect to reap the results we desire. This is a law established by the Maker of the universe, and it is only by complying with it that we can advance towards our goal in life. If we wanted to accomplish things an easier way, we should have to create another world, one in which cooling clouds—for instance—are not preceded by scorching winds.

There is no doubting the fact that failure in life usually results from the quest for immediate success. The word "short-cut" may be applicable to the world of roads and footpaths, but there are no short-cuts in the struggles of life. This fact frequently evinces itself in untoward ways.

Take the instance of a young man in the town of Surat, in Gujarat, who entered a jeweller's shop, stole a piece of jewellery, then tried to make a quick exit. His line of retreat to the staircase being cut off by a suspicious shopkeeper, he made a dash for the nearest window and crashed his way—as he thought—to freedom. But this bold attempt ended disastrously. His leap from the second floor window resulted in his instant death (*The Times of India,* January 21, 1980).

This might appear to be just an isolated incident involving a foolhardy youth, but one finds people generally considered to be intelligent committing the same mistake in their lives. When an individual tries to accomplish instantly what should be worked for over a long period—like the youth who sought to reach ground level by jumping out of a window instead of walking down the stairs—he is condemning himself to destruction. When the leaders of a nation do likewise, their actions spell doom for all those follow their lead.

Making the Extra Effort

Lee Iacocca was born in 1924 to a poor family who had left their home-town in Italy for America in search of a livelihood. Iacocca worked hard at his studies and secured a master's degree in engineering, after which he took a job in the Ford Motor Company, where he continued to rise until he became its President. Later, following some disagreement with Henry Ford II, he was asked to leave the Ford Company in 1978.

Iacocca then got a job in another motor company, the Chrysler Corporation, as its President. This company had gone bankrupt at the time he joined it, running at a loss of almost $ 160 million. He made a proper assessment of the situation, then began to work really hard at improving matters. Within three years he had not only paid back all loans, but was running the company at a profit. Now he takes pride in saying, "I'm the company."

Iacocca subsequently wrote his auto biography which contains many valuable suggestions, based on his experiences, such as "The key to success is not information. It's people. And the kind of people I look for to fill top management posts are the eager beavers. These are the guys who try to do more than they are expected to."

Doing more than is expected of one is the way of sincere and active people. Those who work in this way will surely have greater success in life than they ever expected.

Big-Heartedness

The first Umayyad Caliph, Mu'awiya, was ruling in Damascus. Most of the eastern Byzantine empire had been conquered by Islam. The Caesar had been forced to withdraw to Constantinople, and hold out there. Yet he made incursions into Muslim territory. In one clash the Romans imprisoned some Muslims, one of whom was a man belonging to the Quraysh. When the Caesar learnt of this, he asked for the captives to be brought before him.

The Muslim captives were brought into the Caesar's court with their hands tied and feet in chains. The emperor addressed them disparagingly. "The punishment for such as you will be a slow death. It will be a lesson to you and you compatriotes to stop encroaching upon our territory."

The emperor's words wounded the Qurayshi's sense of honour, and he answered back in a severe tone. "As long as you remain an enemy of Islam," he said, "there will be no peace between us. The price of our blood is a cheap one to pay for death in the path of God. But how precious our blood becomes when it is spilled by a worthless ruler like you."

A patriarch of the Caesar's court became incensed on hearing the Qurayshi's words. He came up and hit the Muslim captive on both sides of the face. The Qurayshi's hands being tied, he could offer no resistance. What he did was cry out in a loud voice: "Mu'awiya, where are you now? Are you not going to take revenge on these dastardly people who have stricken a man of noble birth—one of your own household?" Then he looked towards the patriarch. "I swear by God that there will come a day when you will realize who I am."

Mu'awiya was greatly aggrieved when news of this incident reached Damascus. He resolved to do something to make amends for what had happened. First of all, he arranged an exchange of prisoners with the Byzantine emperor. So great was his determination to secure the release of his men that he agreed to free a greater number of Roman soldiers in exchange for them.

Once the captives had returned home, Mu'awiya surreptitiously hatched a plot. He obtained the services of a man of Syria, a merchant who knew the Roman language. Mu'awiya gave him a great quantity of gold and money, charging him with the task of arresting the patriarch and bringing him to Damascus.

The Syrian travelled as a merchant from Damascus to Constantinople. Before long he had established the identity of the patriarch and made friends with him, wooing him with gifts of perfumes, jewels, silk and other such precious items. The Syrian made several trips between the two cities, bringing the patriarch gifts each time. The whole operation was conducted in the utmost secrecy, with no one learning of it save Mu'awiya, and the merchant himself.

A lengthy period elapsed. Contacts between the two men became so close that the patriarch requested certain specific gifts, which the Syrian promised to bring. On his return to Damascus, he purchased a swift camel and, along with a camel driver, brought it to a place near Constantinople. He himself went on to meet the patriarch. "I have brought all your gifts," he told the Roman, "let's go and collect them." Thus he contrived to take the patriarch to where the camel and his companion were waiting. There both men caught hold of him, tied his hands and feet and, setting him upon the camel, set off towards Damascus.

In this way the patriarch was brought before Mu'awiya. The caliph called a large meeting, to which the captive was also summoned. The Qurayshi who had been struck by the Byzantine courtier was astonished to see his antagonist appear from behind a curtain. "Cousin," Mu'awiya said to his fellow Qurayshi, "now is the time for you to be thankful to this Syrian. He has done exactly as I told him to, without the slightest omission. His efforts have enabled you to extract your right from the patriarch, without wronging him."

"If I had not sworn an oath," said the Qurayshi, "I would have forgiven him." Raising his hand, he struck the patriarch once. "That suffices," he said. "I am pardoning him what remains to be done by way of punishment."

"You are our guest for three days," Mu'awiya told the patriarch. When the three days were over, he was allowed to return to Constantinople, along with the Syrian and the presents he had been promised. Afterwards, all the Roman patriarchs gathered before the Caesar. They advised him not to mistreat Muslim prisoners from now on. "I have not seen any people as respectful, generous and good-natured as they are," said the patriarch who had been their guest. "If Mu'awiya had wanted to imprison me, he could have done so; but that was not his wish."

(*Al-Dawah*, Mecca, 14 Jamad al-Ula, 1405 AH)

There is Always a Way

You have probably seen manufacturers of glass frames scoring the surfaces of sheets of glass with a pen-like instrument, then neatly snapping them into two. The cutting edge of this tool is made up of small razor-edged diamonds. Even the huge drills used for boring through hundreds of feet of rock strata in the search for oil are fitted with diamond cutting edges. It is the extreme hardness of the diamond which makes these tools so effective. The diamond is, in fact, the hardest known naturally-occurring substance. It cannot even be scratched. Put it in acid, and there will be no effect. But there is another aspect to this wonderful stone. If it is heated to a very high temperature it will disappear—it will simply sublimate into carbon dioxide, and if struck a sharp blow at exactly the right point, it will break asunder. You have only to look at diamond gemstones to see what exquisite, multi-faceted forms they can be given by jewellers, because, by studying the inner structure of the diamond, they know exactly where and how to break them.

Similarly, when we find ourselves in difficult situations, we should study them carefully, in the way that the jeweller studies his diamond. We should not approach them, carelessly,

from the strongest point, but with circumspection, from the weakest. We should not adopt methods which are likely to gain poor results, like aggessiveness or violence, for these only engender bitterness and obstinacy in others. We should resort to politeness and diplomacy—eschew harsh language in favour of gentleness and tact.

We should consider also that there are certain human beings who are known as "rough diamonds." That is, on the outside they appear to be unattractive and without merit, whereas on the inside they are of great worth. To bring out their worth, so that their true value is apparent to society, it is pointless scratching at the surface or using acid. If the upright human soul is to be revealed in all its beauty it must be given the same delicate handling and treated with the same expertise as the master craftsman lavishes on a superb but fragile piece of jewelry.

Proceeding with Caution

When rivers have to be crossed, small animals can swim across and larger lightweight animals can swiftly walk across. But watch an elephant who is about to make the crossing. He does not step out briskly like other creatures. First he tests the riverbed for hardness or softness, making sure not to put his whole weight on his forefoot, then, when he is sure of his ground, he sets forth. Even once launched, his progress is slow, for he is still afraid of becoming irremediably stuck in soft mud. He proceeds with caution, testing the riverbed at every step.

Who taught the elephant to do this? Surely it must have been God who gave him his instinct for survival, thus setting upon him His seal of divine approval. God has given us this example to show us that when there are signs of danger in our path, we should not advance carelessly, but should move with similar caution, gauging the nature of the "ground ahead".

Man is endowed with far greater brain power than the elephant. No one lights a fire near reserves of gun powder. No engine driver is careless in shunting petrol bogies. But most of us tend to forget that this is a principle to be followed in social life. Every society is comprised of a variety of people who create different types of environment. In every society there are 'marshy places', there is 'petrol' there are 'thorns' and there are 'pits'. The wise are those who try to avoid such difficult, even explosive situations, thus saving themselves from the trammels of confrontation.

Those who have some goal or the other before them never allow themselves to become enmeshed in such things because that would mean being diverted from their objective. A purposeful man always looks ahead to the future,—straight forward and not towards, right or left. He always thinks of long-lasting consequences rather than momentary considerations. He looks at things not from the point of view of personal desires and whims, but from the point of view of reality.

The First Emigration

By the fifth year of the Prophet Muhammad's mission, conditions in Mecca had become intolerable for many of the Muslims, as persecution by the Quraysh intensified. At this time the Prophet advised his companions to emigrate to Abyssinia. This is called the first emigration of Islam; it preceded by some eighty years the mass emigration of Muslims to Medina.

This was part of the advice which the Prophet imparted to his followers on the occasion of the emigration to Abyssinia:

> "Disperse in the land; surely God will gather you once again."

How meaningful these words of the Prophet are! What they amount to is an exhortation by the Prophet to his followers that they should avoid confronting the enemy for the present, but rather remove themselves from the line of fire. God would then provide them with the means to vanquish the enemy; He would gather them together so that they could come into their own once again.

Emigration is indeed a great test of patience. It is those who pass this test who will receive the reward of God. As the Prophet said: "You should know that succour comes with patience; there is ease with hardship."

Patience, then, is the ladder by which one ascends to the Lord's favour and succour. It is with patience that we should react to the difficulties of life, for it is on the field of human patience that divine succour descends. Our ability to face hardship with patience is a great portent, for it means that we are leaving our cause to God. That is a signal for the swift ending of our plight, and the conversion of our hardship into ease.

Real paradise lies on the other side of the divide of patience. Any paradise that one finds without crossing that divide can only be an illusion.

Muslim Journalism

The first generation of Muslims were moved by a sense of discovery. But present generation Muslims base their efforts on a feeling of loss. This is the basic reason for all the intellectual and ethical differences between latter-day Muslims and the original Islamic community.

For those became Muslims at the opening of the Islamic era, Islam was the greatest of blessings. But present-day Muslims have no such feeling for their faith. All they have is a feeling that other nations have taken away from them the political supremacy that Islamic history had granted them. It is for this reason that Muslims the world over are today suffering from a persecution complex. They look at other nations as oppressors and themselves as the oppressed. They hold different nations responsible for their problems in various parts of the world.

America, Israel, and Russia are variously the target of their anger and resentment. The Jews, Hindus, and Christians, are held responsible at different moments for their plight. Because of this attitude, all they have been able to achieve through their efforts has been futile protest.

This has also had an adverse effect on Muslim journalism. There is one thing common to the Muslim press the world over, and that is protest. All Muslim periodicals and newspapers today have adopted this tone. Their sole purpose is to put forward the Muslims' political case. But the true purpose of Muslim journalism should be to represent Islam; it should be run on the basis of principle, not on the basis of national prejudice.

If one represents a nation's case, one will spotlight its national issues. But to represent Islam, on the other hand, is to present God's religion before mankind. The Qur'an tells us how God sent countless prophets in ancient times, and revealed to them the scriptures. Man, however, was unable to preserve these scriptures in their original form. Then the final Prophet came to the world. The Book that was revealed to him would be preserved for all time. It is now our responsibility as Muslims to communicate this authentic book of divine guidance to all nations and all peoples of the world. True Muslim journalism is that which represents the message of Islam in this way.

A Practical Solution

"When one's ego is touched," an eminent psychologist once observed, "it turns into super-ego, and the result is breakdown." Much the same thing was said some thirteen hundred years back by 'Umair ibn Habib ibn Hamashah. During his last days this Companion of the Prophet Muhammad gave some advice to his grandson, Abu Ja'afar al-Khatmi, part of which was about patience. "One who does not bear with a small hurt from a foolish person will have to bear with great harm," was what he said.

The gist of both these remarks is the same, namely that the only way to avoid being harmed by others is to keep out of their firing line as much as possible, to keep as far away as one can from those who show themselves to be potentially harmful.

Every human being is born with an "ego". More often than not, that ego is dormant. It is better to leave it sleeping, for the ego can be like a snake which, when aroused, will harm all within its reach.

It is a commonplace in any society for one to be put out, and even aggrieved, as a result of someone else's foolishness or willful malice. Usually the best way of avoiding great harm from mischief-makers is to put up with initial hurt, for, if one does not, one will set off a chain reaction in which things will go from bad to worse. Instead of having to bear a relatively small hurt, one will be subjected to much greater suffering. And if one has not been able to bear a pelting with stones, how will one fare when great rocks descend upon one's head?

The Will to Unite

If an engine driver is to set his locomotive in motion, he has to stand before the fire and endure it is fierce heat. This huge and complex machine, built up of so many parts, will remain immobile unless he is prepared to do so. The same goes for society. It will not function unless the individuals who have to make all its parts work are prepared to sacrifice something of their own and are ready to endure difficulties, if not actual hardship. And just as all the moving parts of a locomotive have to be kept regularly oiled, if they are not to be worn out with friction, thus bringing the machinery to a standstill, so tolerance must be a feature of society, if it is to function as a harmonious whole. Tolerance is the oil which will let the wheels go round. There can be no teamwork without it.

When people work together in groups, it is inevitable that there should be disagreements and that complaints should be voiced. However well-intentioned the individuals concerned may be, such negative feelings are bound to surface sooner or later. How is it possible then to work together in harmony? There is only one way, and that is to make a considered decision to remain united in the face of disagreement. It is a question of individuals being conscious of the necessity for harmony, and willing themselves to take complaints in their stride, if they are unjustified, and to start the process of self-examination, if the grounds for complaint have any validity in even the smallest measure. This is not asking for the impossible. Who does not do exactly this in his family life as a matter of good sense and practicality? When family members are living in close proximity, grievances do arise and tempers often flare up. But family cohesion is not destroyed because of this, for blood relationships prevent such feelings from getting out of hand. Grievances are swept away by mutual love, and tempers are cooled by words of regard and affection. And so the unity of the family remains intact. The home, indeed, is a microcosm of social existence. It provides a day-to-day working model of social harmony unflawed by grievances or disagreement.

The feelings of love which cement family life can be brought into being in social life through conscious deliberations. Unity can spring from a human awakening to its ultimate necessity.

Where family life is governed by the heart, social life is governed by the will. There is nothing that cannot be endured for the sake of unity, provided there is the will to achieve it.

Doing One's Bit

There was once a man who stubbornly refused to believe that it is God who provides for and nourishes his creatures. His friends did their best to make him understand this, but with no success. Finally, he decided to silence them by putting this notion to the test. Leaving his home early one morning, he went off to a jungle where he perched himself up in a tree. "If it is God who nourishes His servants, He will send me my food here too," he thought.

He sat in the tree the whole day, but there was no sign of any food. After going without breakfast, lunch and dinner, he was all the more convinced that such ideas were all nonsense. He was about to go home when he saw some wayfarers searching for a tree they could pass the night under. They finally chose the very tree in which he was perched. He decided not to reveal his presence and just watched what was going on at the base of the tree. After setting up their camp, they took themselves off to collect firewood, and having done this they, opened their bags and took out rice and pulses to cook a meal. When it was nearly ready, they threw a handful of chillies into the hot oil to season it. Such a spicy aroma rose up into the air that the man in the tree sneezed. Only then did the travellers learn of his presence, whereupon they invited him to share what they had cooked.

The man happily went back home and said to his friends the next morning, "What you said was quite true. But you hadn't told me the whole story. Of course, God does provide you with food. It's just that you have to sneeze and come down a tree to get it!"

Although humorous in tone, this little anecdote is serious in intent. It is, in fact, a parable which underscores the notion that God helps those who help themselves. And although man's role is a very minor one, it is nevertheless a very necessary one. A man must prove his worth to have his due share of God's gifts. We must never, therefore, neglect to make ourselves deserving of God's nourishment.

Broken Pledges

Once a doctor was visited by a stranger who had a box with him. He sat in a corner waiting until all the patients had gone, and the doctor was left alone, then with an air of secrecy he opened up the box in front of the doctor. It contained a gold necklace. The stranger told him that this chain was worth Rs 10,000, but hastened to add that he did not want to sell it. He only wanted to borrow Rs 5000 against it. He had run into great difficulties and had felt forced to pawn something valuable. He said that he would be very grateful if the doctor could give him enough money to see him through this emergency. He promised to come back in one month's time and redeem the necklace. The doctor at first said that he was not interested, and refused to give him any money. But the man persisted, explaining his plight in such a piteous way that the doctor softened and agreed to help him out. He handed over the money, then locked the chain in his safe.

Month after month elapsed, but there was no sign of the man returning. The doctor began to feel apprehensive. Then one day he decided to take the necklace out of his safe and send it to a jeweller to have it valued, so that he could sell it. To his consternation he was told that it was made of brass. Although the doctor was shocked momentarily, it did not take him long to recover. He said that he had lost his money but that he would not lose his composure. He chose to forget all about this sad incident, and simply took the chain out of his safe and put it in a common almirah, along with other articles made of brass.

This attitude adopted by the doctor is the best solution to many problems that arise from our contacts with other people. Whenever our hopes and trusts have been betrayed, we feel that we have genuine grounds for feeling aggrieved. When a supposed man of principle proves a scoundrel, a well-wisher turns out an enemy and a reasonable person shows himself to be quite the reverse, we feel really let down.

On such occasions, the best policy is to bring those who have disappointed us down from the high pedestals that we had them on, and put them back among the commonplace. What had formerly been considered 'gold' should then be accepted as being only 'brass' and given a place accordingly. This is the only way to retain one's equanimity in the face of life's many disappointments.

Dreams and Success

Mr. Ram Ratan Kapila runs a refrigerator and air-conditioner business by the name of Kapsons, its offices being located in Asaf Ali Road in New Delhi. Needing a catchy name for his firm, he advertised for one in the newspapers, promising a handsome reward for the best slogan. In spite of repeatedly advertising, no apt slogan was forthcoming. He kept racking his brain day in and day out, but could not hit on anything that sounded just right.

Six whole years came and went, then one night Mr Kapila dreamt he was in a beautiful garden, with birds chirruping and perfect weather. Delighted with his surroundings, he exclaimed, "What wonderful weather!" It had taken him six years, but he had found the right catch phrase at last:

Kapsons: the weather masters.

The dream is an activity which goes on in the sleeping state inside the mind, often crystalling unformed thoughts and desires. Often what has been going on during the day appears in dreams at night. History abounds in tales of discoveries which have been made through dreams, and problems, which had apparently been insoluble, being happily solved on wakening from an illuminating dream sequence. An inventor's mind, when totally engrossed in his invention, continues to project the ins and outs of the problems even when he is asleep. It is not unusual for answers to seemingly impossible questions to appear in the course of dreams. But this only happens as a result of total intellectual association with any given subject. Success is the result of devotion and assiduity, and is never the result of some unasked for miracle.

Ethics and Technology

Soon after the completion of a multi-storeyed building called Akashdeep in Bombay, the whole construction collapsed. The engineers said that the reason for its collapse was that less cement had been used than specified by safety regulations.

In another statement the director of a technical institute said, "RCC construction is a scientific process which is excellent in the hands of qualified and experienced people, but dangerous if managed by incompetent engineers and contractors." *The Times of India*, 4 September, 1983)

This appears to be the correct and proper explanation of the matter, but if we really think about the word 'incompetent' as applied to the engineers and contractors concerned, we realize that it needs to be replaced by the more appropriate word 'corrupt'. The truth is that such problems in this country are traceable to excessive greed and corruption, and not to a lack of technical expertise.

The Bhakra Dam being a major government project, the services of the top engineers were obtained for its construction. But, no sooner was it ready than its walls began to crack, costing the government crores of rupees to rebuild.

Such events are frequent in this country. Despite all such ventures being supervised by technical experts, one hears of roads falling into disrepair the moment they are constructed, of buildings needing to be repaired almost immediately after being built, and of plans remaining incomplete even after projects are 'completed.' All this is the result of corruption and has nothing to do with a lack of technical expertise.

Corruption is a psychological evil, while lack of skill is a technical shortcoming. A psychological evil cannot be removed by technical improvement. If we are genuinely interested in making a better society in our country, we shall have to work for the psychological, or moral reform of the individuals who comprise the nation. Merely bringing about an increase in the number of technical courses available will not make them turn over a new leaf.

The More Hurry, the Less Speed

An Indian Airlines Airbus, flight IC 406, from Bombay to Delhi, left Bombay half an hour behind schedule. Soon after the take-off, one of the passengers sent a note to the pilot, Captain Bhatnagar, asking him the reason for the delay in departure. The latter asked him to come to the cockpit so that he could explain the position to him.

The passenger not only refused to be convinced, but hit captain Bhatnagar from behind saying:

"I have seen many pilots like you!"

Upset over the incident, Captain Bhatnagar decided to return to Bombay 25 minutes after the take-off. This naturally led to strong protests from the other passengers. Later, the Indian Airlines arranged for another crew to take the flight to Delhi. The net result? The flight reached Delhi over three hours late.

This is an example of how important it is to adopt a patient attitude in life. The above-mentioned passenger refused to put up with a delay of half an hour, and, as a result, he had to wait for three hours. Had he remained patient about the half-hour delay, he would have certainly saved himself the trouble of waiting for three hours.

Further, according to the report, a high-level inquiry has been ordered into the incident by the Airlines.

No matter what the result of the inquiry, it is certain that the passenger will have to sacrifice more of the thing he had wanted to save—time.

God Helps Those Who Help Themselves

A young aspiring Muslim student from Azamgarh, A.M. Khan by name, stood nervously before the Principal of Hindu College. "Sir, I should very much like to be admitted to the B.Sc. course in your college." The reaction was sharp. "The admissions are closed. How do you expect to be admitted in the month of October when you are already several months late with your applications." Unforeseen circumstances had prevented young Khan from applying sooner, but he simply said, "It would be extremely kind of you if you would help me." Then he added hesitatingly, "One whole year will be wasted for me if I am not granted admission." The Principal's reply was stern. "There is just no question of further admissions."

The principal talked in such an offhand manner that it should have been obvious that there was no point in persisting. Even so the student was determined to try his luck, although all he really expected was to be asked to leave the room immediately. On seeing the insistence of the student, the principal finally asked him rather drily what his marks had been in the previous examinations, because he felt certain that he must have failed to get admission elsewhere due to his low marks. If this were the case, the principal would have had good grounds for rejecting his application. But the students's reply was just the opposite of what he expected. He said, "Eighty five percent, sir."

These words worked like a miracle. The principal's mood changed all of a sudden, and he asked the student to sit down and show him his certificates. When he had seen them and was satisfied that the student's claim was true, he told him to write out an ante-dated application.

Not only was the student then given admission in spite of such a long delay in applying, but he was also granted a scholarship by this very same principal who had been so reluctant even to give him a hearing.

Had the same student approached the principal with a third class degree, and had been refused admission as a result, he would surely have gone away full of hatred for the principal concerned, and would have remarked to his friends that it was prejudice which had come in his way. He would not have admitted that he had been refused admission because of his poor results. He would have publicly understood by aspirants to high positions that the response of the society we live in is usually an echo of our own condition. We tend to attribute the evils afflicting us to society so that we may shake ourselves free of the blame.

When a man enters life fully prepared to meet its challenges, the world cannot but give him due recognition. Never in any environment does he fail to receive the position of honour which is his due. This results in his being able to maintain high moral standards. His conduct is then marked by bravery, confidence, broad-mindedness, gentlemanliness, acknowledgement of others' worth and a realistic approach to life. He has the will and the capacity to enter into proper human relationships. Society having recognized his talents and he in turn having given due acknowledgement to society, he can rise above the negative attitudes of hatred and prejudice.

The reverse is true when, because he cannot come up to the required standards, he fails to prove his worth; when he enters life with inadequate training he surely fails to find a place of his choice in the world. As a depressed personality, he almost certainly develops a low moral character. He falls a prey to negative psychology—anger, complaint, even criminality. Failure in life gives birth to this negative psychology, because it is seldom that the person concerned blames himself for his failure. He almost always lays the blame on others for his own shortcomings. Inadequate preparation for life brings two evils simultaneously—failure on one's own part and uncalled-for complaint against others.

A stone is hard to all and sundry. But it presents no problems to anyone who has a tool which can break it. The same is true of the more complex obstacles that face us in life, for it is only if you enter the field of life equipped with the proper skills, that you feel entitled to claim what is your due. Even after the "last date" you can be given admission to a college without anyone else intervening to help you. But without the necessary skills and ability, you will fail to find the place you truly deserve.

Anyone who wants success to come his way in this world of God will first have to make himself deserving of it. He must know himself and his circumstances. He must organize and channelise his energies properly. He must enter the field fully armed in every respect, then others cannot fail to recognize his true value. He must be like the tree which forces its way up through the undergrowth to take its place in the sun.

Negligence: A Moral Deficiency

It is hard to believe that any animal could be more dangerous or terrifying than the man-eating tiger. But it is not the tiger or the bear which is the most dangerous enemy of man. In truth, the most dangerous of our enemies are the bacteria which are so tiny that they remain invisible to the naked eye. Small they may be, but these bacteria breed at such a furious rate that, given favourable conditions, one of their number can reproduce itself 10,000 times over within a mere matter of ten hours. While a bear or a lion only occasionally eats a man alive, man is the constant focus of deadly bacteria.

Their species run into thousands. We are fortunate, however, in that 99 percent are either beneficial or harmless. Though only one percent is harmful, its deadliness is such that it can claim the life of a man within a matter of seconds. All fatal diseases, according to medical science, are produced by such micro-organisms. Their very lack of bulk makes it possible for them to enter the human system in ways against which man has no natural system of defence.

People are usually aware of big and obvious dangers, and imagine they must be responsible for all their misfortunes. But, if the truth were told, the harm done to us by these tiny living organisms far surpasses any havoc our bigger enemies can wreak. Yet, when we come to think of it, the greatest damage of all is done by those seemingly insignificant and often short-lived moments of neglect—moments when timely action was our duty, when approval needed to be given or withheld, when advice or help or self-appraisal was needed, and we let the occasion slip by, heedless of the consequences. Easy-going negligence can creep into our souls, like bacteria into the body, and, if not pulled up short, can become an ingrained attitude, leading to moral corrosion.

A negligent attitude permits people to fritter away their time, day after day, with no thought for the future.

Similarly, they squander substantial portions of their income. This wasted time and pointless expenditure may seem a trivial matter, if it is just a question of one day—a few hours and a few rupees don't seem to add up to much. But if one were to calculate the time and money thus wasted in one year and then in a whole lifetime, it would become clear that fully fifty percent of one's life and earnings had been squandered in vain pursuits. Take the total wastage of a whole nation and the loss assumes such enormous proportions that it quite goes beyond the imagination.

A Lesson from a Tiger

Jim Corbett, after whom a famous national park in India has been named, was an expert on the nature of tigers. He once wrote: "No tiger attacks a human being unless provoked." People who live in jungle areas where tigers roam will confirm the truth of Jim Corbett's words. There is usually no cause for concern when one comes face to face with a tiger. Unless it is provoked—or harbours deep-rooted suspicion of human beings—the beast will ignore one and continue on its way.

And how does this suspicion form in some tigers? Tigers are by nature not ill-disposed towards human beings. Only very few of them can be called man-eaters, and even they were not born as such. They became man-eaters, not through any fault of their own, but through the folly of human beings. Usually it is inexperienced hunters who do the damage. They shoot at a beast, wounding but not killing it. A tiger injured in this manner becomes man's enemy. Wherever it sees a human being, it attacks and kills. The same is true of most beasts of prey. They only attack man when they have already been wounded by him.

This information from the world of nature holds deep significance for man. It shows that one should not think of anyone—not even the most savage people—as one's enemy in advance. One will only be treated as an enemy if that is how one sees others. If one does not view them with animosity, they are more likely to be amicable in return.

The second lesson is that one should not take measures against anyone without sufficient preparation. If the measures that one takes are indecisive, they are sure to be counter-productive. The other party will only become further provoked, and tension between the two will deepen further.

Everyone has certain needs and desires in this world, which they remain busy fulfilling. The secret of life is not to stand in a person's way. If one does not make oneself a target for another's vengeance, but lets everyone continue pursuing his own goal in life, then one is not going to find one's own path blocked by others. One will find everyone so asborbed in minding his own business that he has no time to interfere with that of others.

Realizing One's Own Shortcomings

He had reached old age and was still unmarried. When asked his reason for remaining a bachelor, he said that he had always been looking for a perfect spouse. "But in all this time, did you not find one?" he was asked. "Once I did," he replied, "but unfortunately she was looking for a perfect spouse too, and I did not come up to the required standard."

Generally people are expert at detecting the faults of others. That is why they are unable to get on with anybody. If they were to seek out their own faults, instead of those of others, they would realize that they are in the same position as they find others to be in. Awareness of one's own shortcomings makes for a spirit of humility in individuals and unity in society. If one sees only the faults of others, on the other hand, one will become arrogant, and perennially be at odds with one's fellows.

It is a fact of psychology that no single person can be an amalgam of all good qualities. Just as there are many shades of grey between black and white, so are there many gradations of good and evil in ordinary human beings. While few are saints, few also are the out-and-out villains of this life, and many are the combinations of different qualities and defects than one can find in any given individual. It is no simple matter to label a person wholly good or wholly bad. If there is to be harmony within a community, the bad sides of its members must be tolerated, while their good sides are appreciated. In this way, no talent is lost to society, and fellow-feeling will prevail. This is a principle that should be remembered in all life's relationships. Man and wife, employer and employee, businessman and partner—all need to keep it in mind. If we want to pluck "flowers," we have also to bear the "thorns" that come with them. There is no way that one who cannot put up with thorns will be able to possess the flowers of this life.

There are few great tasks which can be accomplished by individuals single-handedly. Only the talents of several individuals combined can achieve any substantial work. Just as this is true in commercial and political spheres, so is it true of religious work also. But in whatever field work is going on, people will only be able to work together if they are patient and tender-hearted in their outlook. They will have to bear with one another, putting ill-feeling behind them, not becoming alienated towards one another over petty issues. It is all very well to be an idealist, but if one eternally seeks the ideal in people, one is bound to be disappointed. The only way to be able to work with others, then, is to overlook the fact that they do not come up to one's ideal standard, and even to extend moral support to those who seem the most deficient.

Character Builds the Nation

Toyota, a Japanese motor company, has been functioning for the last thirty years without a single day ever having been wasted, and without its production ever once having slackened. This is only one of the many examples which explain the fast development of industry in Japan. General Motors and the Ford Motor Company of the U.S.A. are the biggest motor manufacturing companies in the world. The annual production of these motor companies is, on an average, 11 cars per employee, while the Toyota Motor Company annually produces 33 cars per worker.

Considering the non-existence or at least paucity of all the major raw materials of industry in Japan—coal, iron, petroleum, etc.,—Japan still manages to surpass all other countries in industrial progress. One might well ask why. A *Hindustan Times* commentator (25 August, 1981) attributes Japan's success to "A national spirit of compromise and co-operation, and a willingness to endure short-term setbacks for the long-term good of the nation, company or family."

It is temperament then which plays the most crucial role in the making of a nation. It is important in nation-building in the way that bricks are important in any kind of construction work. A house made of unfired bricks is unsafe, because any calamity, even a minor one, can bring it tumbling down. A building, on the other hand, which is made of kiln-fired bricks can be trusted to withstand the onslaught of tempests and floods.

A character so tempered that it can be depended upon through thick and thin—like the kiln-fired brick—is what in the long run builds a nation, for it is only such a temperament which can remain attuned to the more and more complex procedures of industrialization and remain steadfastly geared to national progress.

How to Lead, Even in Defeat

In 1827 A.D., the Mediterranean island of Sicily became part of the growing Islamic empire. For nearly three hundred years it remained under Islamic rule. Then, in 1090, it was reconquered by the Normans.

The founder of the Norman kingdom of Sicily was Roger II (1095-1154). In 1110 he succeeded his brother as count of Sicily and in 1130 was crowned king. Although he belonged to a nation of conquerors, and it was the Muslims whom he had defeated, he still retained a high respect for Arabs and Islam. His coronation mantle was designed by a Muslim artist, and had Arabic inscriptions woven into it. After his coronation, he decided that he would like to have a chart showing the full extent of the Norman empire. He chose a Muslim cartographer, Al-Idrisi, to design this chart, for he was the greatest expert in the field. Al-Idrisi then went on to prepare an atlas for the king, consisting of seventy maps and extensive geographical data. Originally written in Arabic, the first European edition of this atlas was published in 1619.

The selection of Al-Idrisi for the mammoth task of preparing maps of the whole of the known world shows, as the historian J.H. Kramers has pointed out, that at that time the intellectual and academic superiority of Muslims was accepted by one and all. Roger II certainly appreciated the worth of Muslim scholars: he encouraged and sponsored them in their work and—in the words of one historian —"made Sicily a major meeting place for Christian and Arab scholars."

Though defeated on the field of battle, Muslims continued their intellectual and academic dominance, even in the court of their conqueror. This was because at that time Muslims were far and wide the most advanced race in almost every field of knowledge. The legacy of Islam lives in European languages, which retain many words of Arabic origin.

Muslims today complain of their political, economic and military subjection to non-Muslim nations. They think that they can take back, by protest and militancy, what has been seized from them. But the case of Roger II of Sicily—his respect for Muslim scholars and their continued intellectual domination even after military defeat—shows that the solution to the problems of the

Muslims in the modern age lies in their cultivating technological capability, and establishing dominance in the field of modern scientific knowledge. This can be achieved—not by protests and militant "fundamentalism", but by earnest academic endeavour alone; it can be acquired by seeking to give to the world, rather than just take from it.

History Speaks

Roger II (1095-1154), founder of the Norman dynasty in Sicily, holds a distinguished place among medieval European monarchs. He had his capital at Palermo, and is noted for having made Sicily into a prosperous country. He established a strong administration, and constructed a powerful fleet. The success of Roger II, according to a western historian, can be attributed in part to the fact that he "made Sicily a meeting place of European and Arabic scholars."

Al-Idrisi was a contemporary of Roger II. Born in Marrakesh, he was educated in Spanish universities. Later he travelled extensively in Europe, Asia and Africa. He became the greatest geographer if his age, and a close friend and adviser to Roger II, at whose court he served as official geographer. Roger II originally invited Al-Idrisi to Sicily to make a map of the world for him.

Here we can see the cause of the esteem in which Muslims were held in times past. They made Islam a dominant force on the world scene, not through protests and demands, nor from spreading conflict and terror, but through being useful to the world. By virtue of hard struggle, they established themselves as intellectual leaders of the world. They had something that others did not have, so people flocked to their sides. That was how Muslims raised their standing in the world in times past. It is by the same method that they can improve their position today, and build for a bettor future.

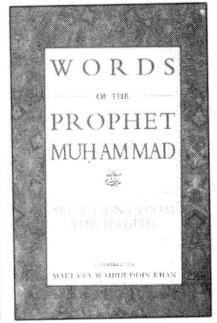

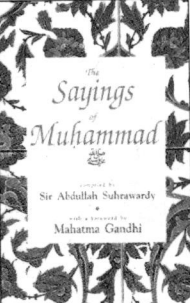

MUHAMMAD
A PROPHET FOR ALL HUMANITY
MAULANA WAHIDUDDIN KHAN

The Wonderful Universe of ALLAH
INSPIRING THOUGHTS FROM THE QUR'AN ON NATURE

WOMAN
BETWEEN ISLAM AND WESTERN SOCIETY
Maulana Wahiduddin Khan

PRESENTING THE QUR'AN

RELIGION and SCIENCE

The Beautiful Promises of Allah

WORDS OF THE PROPHET MUHAMMAD
SELECTIONS FROM THE HADITH
MAULANA WAHIDUDDIN KHAN

THE LIFE OF THE PROPHET MUHAMMAD
MUHAMMAD MARMADUKE PICKTHALL

HIJAB IN ISLAM
Maulana Wahiduddin Khan

The Beautiful Commands of ALLAH

WOMAN IN ISLAMIC SHARI'AH
Maulana Wahiduddin Khan

INDIAN MUSLIMS
The Need For A Positive Outlook
Maulana Wahiduddin Khan

The Sayings of Muhammad
compiled by
Sir Abdullah Suhrawardy
with a foreword by
Mahatma Gandhi

ISLAM
Creator of the Modern Age
MAULANA WAHIDUDDIN KHAN

A TREASURY OF THE QUR'AN
MAULANA WAHIDUDDIN KHAN

ISLAMIC BOOKS

- Islam and Peace
- Principles of Islam
- The Quran for All Humanity
- Indian Muslims
- God Arises
- Islam: The Voice of Human Nature
- Islam: Creator of the Modern Age
- Woman Between Islam and Western Society
- Woman in Islamic Shari'ah
- Islam As It Is
- An Islamic Treasury of Virtues
- Religion and Science
- Man Know Thyself
- Muhammad: The Ideal Character
- Tabligh Movement
- Polygamy and Islam
- Hijab in Islam
- Concerning Divorce
- The Way to Find God
- The Teachings of Islam
- The Good Life
- The Garden of Paradise
- The Fire of Hell
- Islam and the Modern Man
- Uniform Civil Code
- Muhammad: A Prophet for All Humanity
- A Treasury of the Qur'an
- Words of the Prophet Muhammad
- Qur'an: An Abiding Wonder
- The Call of the Qur'an
- The Moral Vision
- Introducing Islam
- The Qur'an
- The Koran
- Heart of the Koran
- The Moral Values of the Quran
- The Basic Concepts in the Quran
- The Essential Arabic
- Presenting the Qur'an
- The Wonderful Universe of Allah
- The Soul of the Qur'an
- Tell Me About Hajj
- The Muslim Prayer Encyclopaedia
- After Death, Life!
- Living Islam
- A Basic Dictionary of Islam
- The Muslim Marriage Guide
- The Beautiful Commands of Allah
- The Beautiful Promises of Allah
- Muhammad: A Mercy to all the Nations
- A-Z Steps to Leadership
- The Sayings of Muhammad
- The Life of the Prophet Muhammad

Goodword
B · O · O · K · S

1, Nizamuddin West Market, New Delhi 110 013
Tel. 462 5454, 461 1128, Fax 469 7333, 464 7980
e-mail: skhan@vsnl.com / goodword@mailcity.com